Transforming Inner Pain: Moving Beyond the Grief and Reclaiming Your Life After Loss

By Kayla Brissi

Copyright

Transforming Inner Pain: Moving Beyond the Grief and Reclaiming Your Life After Loss

ISBN: 978-1-7367397-0-9
Printed in the United States of America
First Printing: July, 2021
Publisher: Highly Favored Publishing LLC

Cover Design: Mariam Abid
Cover: Image @feelartfeelant
Editing: Rebecca Camarena of Rebecca's Author Services

Table of Contents

Dedication

To all those struggling with adversity and experiencing any form of grief and loss resulting from these challenges, I see you and honor your story. May the wisdom and resources within the pages of this book provide valuable insights, opportunities for growth and support you as you learn to move beyond the pain and reclaim your life!

Acknowledgments

To my husband and son, thank you for your support, encouragement, and belief in me in all that I do. I know this can be a wild and crazy ride at times with the late nights typing away on the computer, the stress to meet my deadlines, and the roller coaster emotions that come with writing and publishing a book. I appreciate your patience and understanding while working towards my goals and continuing to leave my mark on the world.

To my dear friend and colleague, Dr. Nicolya Williams, I genuinely believe the stars aligned for us to meet online some years ago, and I am grateful to have you in my corner. My heartfelt thank you for your faith in me, for giving me the motivational pep talk when needed, and for your willingness to write the foreword for this book. Your wisdom is invaluable, and I am blessed to have you share some of it within this book.

To my editor and book coach, Rebecca Camarena, thank you for helping me make this writing dream of mine a reality and for your support over the years. Your friendship, guidance, and expertise are invaluable. I appreciate you.

To my family, friends, colleagues, mentors, I appreciate the lessons, words of encouragement, advice, and support over the years. You've been an integral part of my transformation, journey, and story; thank you.

Foreword

After going through a divorce three years ago I felt like I lost everything. You see my entire identity was tied into that relationship. After some time I decided to go on a personal development journey to discover who I truly was. While I learned a lot and loved the journey, I noticed a lot was missing. I had been trying to do all the things to "feel" healed, but I was not doing the internal work. I learned a lot in this season, but one great takeaway I had was that I could have all the outward attempts, effort, and support in the world, but if I was not taking care of my mindset and energy none of that would truly matter.

Sadly, I learned this the hard way and I am not alone in this. So many women struggle with this same approach. We apply makeup and fancy clothes and try to "effort" our way to healing. Even when we are overwhelmed with the pain we put on the facade and let the world know all is well and we are feeling good even if we are not. It's exhausting and unsustainable.

But we do it because it's what we are taught. We do it because it seems like the right thing to do. We normalize it because we hope if we look good on the outside no one else will notice what we are truly feeling inside.

Truth bomb, healing doesn't work that way, no matter how much convincing you have to do. Grief is something we all face at some time or another. The truth behind it is we experience grief and loss outside of just death and dying and it tremendously impacts us. Instead of recognizing our strength and tuning into our resilience, we often run from it.

You are a lot stronger and more resilient than you give yourself credit for. Sadly resilience is not something we tap into the way we should. Resilience is seen as the capacity to recover quickly from difficulties; toughness. Being resilient doesn't mean that you won't experience difficulty or distress. It means when it comes you already recognize your ability to handle it. Resilience is not a one and done, it's something you commit to regularly. Just like people go to the gym to build muscle, increasing your resilience takes time and intentionality.

Throughout this book, you're going to see why resilience is so important and how you can tap into it.

When I was first asked to write the foreword for *Transforming Inner Pain: Moving Beyond the Grief and Reclaiming Your Life After Loss* I was blown away. Not only for the opportunity but because I knew this was the book I needed all those years ago and I am beyond confident of the impact this book will have on so many other people's lives. We need more conversations on the blend of spirituality and healing and *Transforming Inner Pain* does just that.

It is a progressive, cutting-edge book filled with so much truth and tangible tools you can use for healing. With this book, you're not only learning about grief and loss, but you will in turn have a practical framework for overcoming challenges and tools to bust through blocks. As a professional licensed counselor and certified life and success coach in NLP, EFT, Hypnotherapy, and T.I.M.E. Techniques I have seen grief far too often and in many different forms. I have also seen the tremendous impact it has on our lives. From divorce to death and everything in between grief is devastating and for some debilitating.

Kayla has created this revolutionary approach to give you the tools to take healing back into your own hands.

It's truly mind-blowing.

If you have ever felt alone with grief or loss you my friend picked up the right book because Kayla indeed has a warrior mindset, unheard of inner strength, and an amazing level of faith, which has allowed her to overcome some of life's most significant challenges and through reading this you will feel more heard and held than you have ever felt!

Cheers to your beautiful healing journey!

Dr. Nicolya Williams
10x Best Selling Author
Healing and Mindset Enthusiast
Certified Life and Success Coach, Hypnotherapist, NLP, and EFT Practitioner
nicolyawilliams.com

Introduction

"You may encounter many defeats, but you must not be defeated. In fact, it may be necessary to encounter the defeats, so you can know who you are, what you can rise from, how you can still come out of it." - Maya Angelou

The above quote is one of my absolute favorites by the late Maya Angelou. I feel it's the perfect quote that encapsulates what's within these pages and is a beautiful reminder that things aren't happening to you; they're happening for you.

As difficult as it may be to face adversities in life, it's important to remember that no one is exempt from them, not me, you, or anyone else. It's inevitable; life is going to challenge you!

There will be times in life where you will want to give up because you feel as though you cannot endure the inner pain any longer, and there will be moments where adversities come and go quickly, and it'll feel like nothing more than ripping off a bandaid. However, if you're stuck in the deep dark depths of despair, struggling to find the courage to overcome a challenge, I want to encourage you to dig deep within and find the inner strength you need to pull yourself out of the depths of hell and into the light!

You can and will RISE! You will come out on the other side stronger, wiser, and have a different perspective on life! I believe in you.

It's no secret that I have been through some pretty significant and life-changing events in my life, such as enduring a painful divorce, a 9-year journey to parenthood, the loss of my beloved father, and being diagnosed with a mental illness to name a few. I thought every single experience would break me, but it didn't because I'm still here blazing trails for others and leaving my mark.

Within the pages of this book, you'll learn more about my life story, the challenges I have faced, the grief and loss I experienced from each traumatic event, practical healing methods, and my framework for overcoming adversity, as well as exercises for you to explore. You can read it front to back or choose to read the chapters that will most meet your needs at any given moment.

Know that you are not alone, and you will get through this!

I want to encourage you to embrace the journey you're on, open your mind and heart to see and experience things from a different perspective, be willing to step out of your comfort zone and try new methods for healing and be patient as your life transforms.

May this book be a guide for you when the going gets tough and offers you some inspiration, hope, healing, and transformation. You can and will move beyond the inner pain, heal any grief, and reclaim your life!

With love and gratitude,

Kayla

Disclaimer

The information provided in the book is for general informational purposes only. All information is provided in good faith, however, we make no representation or warranty of any kind, express, or implied regarding the accuracy, adequacy, validity, reliability, availability, or completeness of any information provided.

The information provided is not intended to diagnose or prescribe any treatment for any medical or psychological condition(s), nor does it claim to prevent, diagnose, treat, mitigate, or cure any medical or psychological conditions.

It contains the ideas and opinions of the author and is intended solely to provide helpful information on a variety of subjects. It is solely with the understanding that the author and publisher are not engaged in rendering medical, health, or any other kind of personal professional services in the book.

The reader should consult his or her medical, health, or other competent professional before adopting any of the suggestions in the book with regard to their health.

The author and publisher specifically disclaim all responsibility for any liability, loss, or risk, personal or otherwise, that is incurred as a consequence, directly or indirectly, of the use and application of any of the contents of this book.

Chapter 1 - Facing Adversity

Throughout my life, I have faced adversity, as I am sure you have too. However, I never realized the *gift* I have until I started sharing my store with others—often hearing that I was resilient, mentally tough, and a warrior. Truthfully, I thought everyone could handle challenges similar to me, but apparently, that's not the case.

Therefore, with all of that said, I feel it's important to briefly touch on the adversities I have faced in my life. Let's review some of the most challenging and life-changing experiences of my life to know where I am coming from and that you aren't alone in this journey.

Moving

The summer before I turned 15, my dad's job transferred him, and my family moved from Michigan to Wisconsin. I left behind family, friends I had known my entire life practically, teammates, and so many other important people I cherished to have in my life. So I said goodbye to the people I loved, the town I was proud to be from, and memories, oh so many memories, as I embarked on a new life in Wisconsin.

Three months after moving, I lost my maternal grandmother to Alzheimer's, and six months after her passing, my maternal grandfather transitioned from cancer. My grandparents were an integral part of childhood, and their passing shortly after my family moved was hard on me. Their passing was my first real experience with grief and loss. So naturally, as a teenager, I didn't know how to handle those feelings, so I buried them deep within and moved on with my life the best I could.

Bullying

After our move, I started a new school. I was in the 9th grade and had to learn to adapt to my new surroundings, make friends, and transition into my new life. As a new student, I experienced a wide range of treatment from my peers. Some were elated that I was there and couldn't wait to be my friend, others were indifferent, and then some were straight-up jerks, bullies.

I got picked on for being from the Upper Peninsula (U.P.) of Michigan and talked differently than others with my Yooper slang. Some boys made fun of me for being a late bloomer and smaller chested, and others liked to snap my bra at random while I walked the halls. At one point, it became a problem for some of my peers that I didn't do drugs, smoke, drink alcohol, or spend my weekends partying. I didn't wear expensive "name brand" clothing, nor did I wear a thong that stuck out the top of my pants.

But I was me, and for some, that was not ok.

It was challenging to be a teenager struggling to find my place in this new life of mine. I felt like an outcast, never really fitting in anywhere. Being a teenager has its challenges, let alone figuring out where you belong amongst your peers. I remember feeling like a chameleon; rather than standing out, I chose to blend in to be liked and feel accepted.

At the start of the school year, I lost my maternal grandmother. Then, volleyball season began, and I remember overhearing comments in the locker room from some teammates' about their dissatisfaction with me still starting a game despite missing practice for her funeral. It was hurtful to hear people I thought were my friends be angry with me over something that wasn't within my control.

In the spring, softball season was on the horizon, and tryouts were soon underway. Unfortunately, my grandfather passed, and I missed the tryout due to his funeral. Nevertheless, I made the team and was the starting pitcher. But, again, fellow teammates were upset that I was on the team, let alone the starting pitcher.

Moreover, I won't get into all of the semantics about softball because they're irrelevant, but I more than showed I deserved to be on the team during spring training and had the reputation to back it up as a 1995 Little League World Series participant whose team placed 5th in the world.

It was mind-boggling to me the cattiness I witnessed amongst my peers. I knew there were hurt feelings and jealousy, but I didn't deserve the betrayal either.

The sad thing is it's not like I wanted my grandparents to transition, and I certainly didn't ask them to, but for whatever reason, these peers weren't a fan of me and felt as though I was receiving special privileges. Rather than show me compassion for my loss, they chose to be unkind. I understand we're all just kids, but seriously?

The drama continued throughout my first year at the new school. I attended an overnight party with my friends towards the end of the school year. I thought all was well, and that night I soon realized things weren't. I became the target. Various incidents occurred that night, but the one that hurt the most was when I found my bra and underwear hanging from the ceiling fan in the kitchen for everyone to see while cooking and consuming their breakfast. They ransacked my overnight bag in my sleep and distributed my belongings throughout the house. I was mocked, laughed at, humiliated.

Shortly thereafter that group of people I thought were my friends decided I could no longer be part of their circle. With a snap of their fingers, I was out! Rumors were moving through the halls about me; none of my former friends would speak to me or tell me why I suddenly was put into exile. I was left to fend on my own for the remainder of the school year. I quickly learned to keep to myself because I no longer knew who I could trust and didn't feel like I fit in anywhere anymore.

I spent weekends crying in my room because I was fifteen, had no friends anymore, and no life. I desperately wished I could go back to Michigan.

Fall came, and I was in High School. I wish I could say that my bullying days were over, but alas, they weren't. Over the next three years, I had friends come and go out of my life. I again got kicked out of friend groups, teammates across multiple sports were unkind for various reasons, and rumors spread like wildfire.

As I reflect on my teenage years, I know that there were times I likely fell short. However, I also know that my parents taught me to be kind to everyone, which has always been part of my code of ethics and moral compass. Which makes me wonder why I was a target for all those years?

Truthfully, I have no idea, but what I do know is I haven't forgotten the pain these peers caused me, and despite the pain, I have forgiven them and began a journey to heal the wounds of my past.

Infertility

Fast forward to my twenties, and this decade was a beast. I married young and before my 22nd birthday. Our marriage was blissful, we were living in Florida, and soon after we wed, I convinced my husband to start trying for a baby. We both wanted a large family and joked that because we were both softball/baseball fans, we would have nine kids and create a team of our own.

After six months of trying for a baby and to no avail, I sought the guidance of my gynecologist. After a series of tests and lab work, I learned that I have polycystic ovarian syndrome (PCOS). When I answered my work phone and heard the devastating news about infertility from my doctor, my heart shattered into a million pieces, and that was the first day of my struggle and journey with infertility.

Over the next few years, we shelled out thousands of dollars in our quest to become parents. As a result, I endured multiple surgeries, had painful injections, phlebotomists poked and prodded me so much that I still see the marks on my arms. In addition, I experienced other health issues such as newfound food and seasonal allergies and being diagnosed with mild depression. And that's just a brief summary of what happened over a few years!

Much to our dismay, we never received our blessing, and our marriage became strained. In the end, after seven years of marriage and ten years together, we parted ways and embarked on a new journey as divorcees navigating the single life in our thirties.

Even though our divorce was amicable, there was still inner pain needing some healing. In our ten years together, we endured quite a bit as a young married couple, and truthfully I also thought we would grow old together.

As I reflect on this marriage, I can see now where things went wrong, and there's no one person to blame either. I said and did some things I am not proud of, and rather than help strengthen our marriage, it split us apart. We were kids trying to figure out how to coexist as a couple and deal with life-changing situations. That's part of the catch 22 with infertility. It'll either strengthen your marriage, and it'll be a blessing, or it'll weaken it and be a curse. For us, I believe it was a contributing factor to our demise.

However, despite everything that happened between us, I am grateful that we have a friendship. Why wouldn't we after all that we've been through together? I feel it shows maturity between the two of us that we can be friends, support each other, and want nothing but happiness for the other person. It didn't happen overnight, but we've got to where we are today with time, patience, and healing.

Note: If you are interested in learning more about my infertility struggle and nine-year journey to parenthood, I encourage you to consider reading my chapter, Receiving God's Grace, in the anthology Dust to Salvation: Stories of Grace, Love, and Redemption in the Midst of Jesus Revealing Unexpected.

Parenthood

After my divorce, I reconnected with an acquaintance, and I'll say the rest is history because after a whirlwind romance, we married, and shortly after that, our son was born.

I wasn't looking for a relationship, let alone love after my previous marriage dissolved. I had sworn off all men and planned to enjoy my life as a single lady. My life was in turmoil. I was alone, embarrassed, hurt, and struggling emotionally, mentally, and financially. I was at my version of rock bottom and found myself so far into the hole that I couldn't see the light to crawl out.

All I wanted to do was get my life back on track, regain control, and adjust to life as a single woman. The mere thought of going on a date gave me anxiety. It wasn't part of the plan. However, God works in mysterious ways sometimes, doesn't he? My husband re-entered my life at the right time, and it's as if God was winking at me.

After enduring infertility for nine years and being told by four specialists that I would never conceive without medical assistance, we proved them wrong and conceived naturally. I had a normal and healthy pregnancy despite all the odds stacked against me.

However, life as a new mom was challenging. My son frequently nursed at night, and I wasn't getting enough sleep, so I could barely function. I was breastfeeding and pumping since I worked out of the home full-time. I was also dealing with the stress of being a new mom and the breadwinner for our family. I was struggling.

Shortly after my dad's passing, I noticed an increase in behavioral concerns with our son, who was 2.5 at the time. I wasn't sure if it was to do with grief since he and my late father were close or something else. Therefore, I discussed my concerns with his pediatrician, and she agreed that he should see a behavioral specialist.

We saw the behavioral specialist, and I questioned whether he was having behavioral issues due to grief, if it could be a sensory processing disorder (SPD), or if he was potentially on the autism spectrum. Long story short, the specialist didn't see any signs of "abnormalities" and brushed it off that I was a worried first-time mom.

Each year at his yearly doctor appointment, I brought up the same concerns with his pediatrician. Again, his doctor performed evaluations and assessments, reviewed his milestones, and discussed whether something medically was prevalent with our son—still no warning signs with his medical team as he kept passing their evaluations.

When he went to 3K, his teacher suggested we consider having him tested for autism as she noticed some autism markers. They didn't stand out significantly, but something to be mindful about and discuss how to proceed as a family. We agreed to wait it out and to see if anything would change. When we enrolled him in 4K, all hell broke loose, and my sweet, fun, school-loving child was nowhere in sight. In short, we all struggled.

I eventually asked the school to evaluate him so that I could use it as a resource for further testing with a specialist. Their test indicated he likely had special needs and that getting a more in-depth evaluation by a specialist would be a good idea.

From there, our son underwent several assessments and testing by two different specialists. After three years of questioning the concerns I had with our son, we finally had a diagnosis—the primary ones being autism spectrum disorder (ASD) and attention deficit hyperactivity disorder (ADHD).

Part of me was relieved to have a diagnosis and that my motherly instincts were correct, and the other part of me was angry, but I digress. It's taken me some time to process and accept this diagnosis. There's a lot to being a mother, let alone being one to a child with special needs.

I had to let go of my skewed perception and ideas of motherhood, even grieve a little, and learn to accept a new version of me as a mother. There's nothing "wrong" with my son; he's simply different, and being different is perfectly ok. Are some days challenging? Yes, absolutely! But seeing life through his eyes is rewarding, and it encourages me to see life, the world, through a different lens.

Now, my husband and I are learning to parent differently to accommodate our son's unique needs and navigate life together as we all learn to embrace this chapter of our lives.

Death

As I mentioned previously, I lost my two maternal grandparents in my teens and struggled with their passing. I lost my paternal grandmother less than six months after my divorce, and that too was painful. I cried like a baby at all of their funerals, and to say I was distraught would be an understatement; it hurt like hell. By the time I was 30, I had no living grandparents as my paternal grandfather transitioned when my father was a teenager, and I never had the opportunity to meet him.

Not many people my age can say they've experienced the heartache from grief and loss as I have at a relatively young age.

If that wasn't painful enough, in May 2017, I lost my dad to cancer. To this day, losing him has single-handedly been the most heart-wrenching and challenging thing I have ever had to endure. As much as I tried to keep my life together, it all came crashing down around me. Everything that I spent years repairing and building, crumbled and I was left to pick up the pieces and rebuild.

I experienced what I call a breakdown, and at that moment, when I experienced a real-life reality check, I quickly sought the help of my doctor. Unfortunately, I was diagnosed with recurrent major depression, generalized anxiety disorder, and signs of post-traumatic stress disorder (PTSD).

Before my breakdown, I was ashamed to admit that anything was wrong or that I needed help. The supposedly strong one of the family was struggling emotionally, mentally, physically, and spiritually. I ignored all the signs of a mental illness and chose to bury it all deep within me to avoid acknowledging that I genuinely needed help. I was embarrassed and felt as though I would be letting my father down if I admitted that I was struggling.

Hindsight is always 20/20, so as I reflect on this experience, I cannot help but shake my head in disgust with myself. I'm smarter than that! But when you're in that much pain, you often lack self-control, the inner strength, and discernment to function at your optimal best. It's challenging to see things at face value and think things through clearly. Therefore, in my case, my ego did the work, and it sure did a number on me!

But, as much as it sucked to receive those diagnoses and hit my version of rock bottom, again, I accepted the help, got on medication, and began my healing journey.

Note: If you are interested in learning more about my experience with losing my dad, coping with grief and loss, trauma, and my healing journey, I encourage you to consider reading my book Healing from Grief:

Transform Your Pain Into Purpose and Honor Your Loved One and my chapter, The Blessing of a Grief Stricken Broken Heart, in the anthology The Beauty in My Mess: Stories of Truth, Transparencies and Triumphs (Volume 1).

Mental Illness

Now that you're aware that I suffer from not one but multiple mental illnesses, let me share with you the struggle I endured for over a year (at least) before I mustered up the courage to ask for help.

I lived life on the edge, irritable, lashed out at everyone, and lacked patience. I went through periods where all I would do is sleep to periods where I couldn't. Additionally, I went through periods where I would binge eat and starve myself because I wasn't hungry. As a result, I gained quite a bit of weight and ruined my metabolism. I hated what I saw in the mirror and quite honestly didn't like myself.

I isolated myself from my family. I stayed indoors and avoided people like the plague. I changed my services in my business so I could stay hidden and work behind the scenes rather than talk to people. As a result, I damaged friendships, relationships with colleagues, my family, and my marriage was on the brink of collapsing too.

My life was in shambles, and it was no one's fault but mine, and that was one hard pill to swallow. So, after accepting help for my mental illnesses, I embarked on a journey to find a better way to heal myself from my mental illness and grief and loss. I wanted to get off the pills and take a holistic approach. It wasn't easy, but I am so glad I advocated for myself and followed my intuition!

Roughly six months after starting the medication, I weaned myself off those pills. I focused on holistic and alternative methods and modalities to help me manage my symptoms from depression and anxiety.

I changed my eating habits, used aromatherapy, got into using crystals and leveraging their healing power, and began utilizing mindful meditation, which truly was a game-changer for me. I also started dabbling with energy healing. After my first Reiki session, I became a believer and advocate. So much so that I got certified mere months later.

I still have some challenging days when life gets too much for me to handle, but it is nothing compared to what it once was. With the holistic and alternative healing methods and modalities, I can use them as often or as little as needed, and I love that I'm not dependent on medication. For the record, there is nothing wrong with being on medication, but I knew that wasn't part of my long-term treatment plan. To each is their own.

I'm a supporter of doing what is in your best interest for your health and well-being. Therefore, I encourage you to consider all options. If medication is the right fit for you, great, and if alternative methods are your jam, that's ok too. If you feel combining the two is your perfect match, so be it. You do you! The important thing is for you to be an advocate for your health and well-being and get the support you need.

Note: If you are interested in learning more about my mental health journey, the breakdown that occurred, and the healing I advocate for, I encourage you to consider reading my book Healing from Grief: Transform Your Pain Into Purpose and Honor Your Loved One and my chapter, The Truth Behind the Mask, in the anthology Driven: A Guidebook for Women by Women; To Inspire and Empower.

Spiritual

After the traumatic passing of my late father, I struggled on an emotional, mental, physical, and spiritual level. It broke me.

As I look back on my life and reflect on this experience, I'm now able to find the blessings and be grateful for all the little things. It's a blessing that my dad was here physically with me for 34 years. Do I wish he was still here? Yes, absolutely! I miss him tremendously every day; however, I know he's here with me in spirit.

How can I be so sure he's here in spirit?

Well, after his passing, an awakening started to unfold from within me. This traumatic experience stirred the pot, and like a volcano preparing to erupt, so did I spiritually. I experienced a series of events that were no coincidence. I know that beyond a shadow of a doubt, these spiritual experiences were with my late father.

My first experience was with a Medium who happened to deliver a message from my late father with such accuracy that I immediately burst into tears. There was absolutely no way she could have known anything about my dad or me, yet, it was as if my dad was standing in front of me that afternoon talking to me and giving me one of his lectures. Gosh, I miss those lectures now, even though they annoyed the hell out of me all those years ago.

This first spiritual experience truly opened my eyes to what I could not *see* and started me on a path of spiritual exploration. As a cradle Catholic, I was extremely hesitant because of my upbringing and the church's beliefs. Quite honestly, I had to deconstruct these beliefs and other limiting ones that allowed me to break free and embrace the journey I was taking.

I soon discovered that I was spiritually gifted, and I wrestled with that internally for a while, especially out of fear of judgment, rejection, and ridicule.

I feared what others might do if they discovered my gifts. Would they accept or disown me? I was fearful that someone would take this information and deem me "crazy" because I live with a mental illness. Trust me, they're not linked, but it was something I worried about, and for a good reason. I worried about what my family would think about it, my spouse, clients, colleagues, and friends. I was a wreck!

Being surrounded by conservative Christians who do not believe in a lot of the spiritual work or see it as evil and demonic gave me additional anxiety and something I had to work through. However, once I committed to being open to the spiritual world and accepting my gifts, my life drastically shifted and in a good way!

Therefore, while the inner turmoil and hard lessons learned were unpleasant, I am grateful that I dared to see the blessings in disguise. I found my bravery to accept myself for who I am, my unique gifts, and own my authentic truth. That, my friend, took a lot of deep inner healing work, which at times was painful and extremely challenging, but oh, so worth it!

Note: If you are interested in learning more about my spiritual journey, awakening, and learning to embrace my gifts as a Christian, I encourage you to consider reading my book Healing from Grief: Transform Your Pain Into Purpose and Honor Your Loved One and my chapter, Answering the Call: Accepting My Divine Gifts, in the anthology Embracing the Journey: Inspiring Stories of Hope, Healing and Triumphing over Adversity.

Lastly, there have been other adversities that I have faced over the years as well. Such as losing my full-time job, significant loss of finances, and nearly losing everything, like my home, to substantial business ups and downs where I thought I would need to go back to the corporate world. I honestly never thought I would make it out on the other side and be ok with each adversity, but I did, and so will you.

Perhaps some of these circumstances you too have experienced, and if so, I hope you feel less alone after reading through many of my life's struggles. We are kindred spirits simply navigating life. I am here for you.

No doubt, I have had my fair share of challenges over the years, and it's not to say they were all traumatic, but they all changed me and my life in some way, shape, or form, and with each, I experienced a varying level of grief and loss.

Yes, my friend, grief and loss are not only associated with death as that is a common misconception. In reality, we can experience loss when we experience something traumatic or life-changing. For example, a natural disaster can trigger a loss of safety and security. Likewise, a violent act can be associated with a loss of innocence or hope.

Grief and loss, trauma, and healing are topics that I have become passionate about discussing because of my journey and the adversities I have faced. I feel that it's part of my Divine purpose to support others in a similar position. With that said, let's explore this topic further in the next couple of chapters.

Chapter 2 - Grief and Loss

When we break down the topic of grief and loss, it becomes easier to understand and see its connection with adversity.

Grief is a natural response to loss and is a personal experience for people regardless of where their pain stems from, such as losing a loved one or a loss of good health. I see it as a right of passage that we all experience in this journey of life.

Grief reactions can feel like a direct response to physical causes. For example, the death of a loved one or beloved pet, or through symbolic or social losses, such as divorce, loss of finances, health, independence, or a job.

Each kind of grief represents something lost or taken away from you. While people experience various types of loss throughout their lives, the experience is vastly different and can trigger particular grief reactions. These reactions can be emotional, mental, physical, social, or even spiritual.

For example, psychological reactions, referring to emotional and mental issues, can include:

- Anxiety
- Sadness
- Despair
- Guilt
- Anger

Physical responses may include:

- Changes in appetite
- Weight gain or loss

- Illness
- Sleeping problems

Social reactions typically include:

- Difficulty returning to work
- Self-isolation
- Unwillingness to be around loved ones

Spiritual reactions may include:

- Blaming God
- Distancing yourself from your faith
- Leaving the church

Unfortunately, not addressing grief and loss causes a domino effect where problems compound until you're forced to address the situation.

It's important to also note that no two people experience grief the same. Even if, for example, two siblings lose a parent, their grief journey will be different. We're hardwired differently, and the takeaways from our experiences determine how we move forward and heal.

When we look closely at grief, we encounter stages of grief when we experience loss. Now, before I delve into the stages of grief, it's crucial to understand the following key points:

1. Trauma often includes a feeling of loss.
2. Loss is not always traumatic.
3. Grief can be an experience of loss.
4. Bereavement is the response to a loss.
5. Mourning is the process of adapting to a loss.

Grief is often a wound in need of healing. When a wound is healing, there are stages in its natural healing progression. Therefore, let's discuss these stages with one tiny caveat. The stages of grief include the professional opinion and research of the late Elisabeth Kübler Ross and my own professional opinion and personal experience. My thoughts and personal experiences are not to discredit the late Elisabeth Kübler Ross and her work but to expand upon the concepts with a different lens.

In 1969, Elisabeth Kübler Ross first identified the five stages in her book, *On Death and Dying,* after interviewing terminally ill patients. Per her findings, the five stages she developed associate with those who are dying and include denial, anger, bargaining, depression, and acceptance. Furthermore, other grief experts argue that there are seven stages of grieving: shock, denial, bargaining, guilt, anger, depression, and acceptance.[1]

I feel there are nine stages of grief when experiencing loss yourself, in my personal and professional opinion. When my father transitioned, I can attest to the validity of the seven stages of grief because I experienced them firsthand. However, I do feel that once you reach acceptance, there's also transformation and purpose.

As I reflect on the adversities I have faced throughout my life, I can easily recall several of these stages. Therefore, my next important point to note is that you may or may not experience all nine stages of grief yourself, and no matter which ones you experience, it won't be in a linear fashion. You may even revisit some of them multiple times.

Know that this is your healing journey, and to honor it, don't compare it to someone else's either because it won't be the same, which is why I discuss all nine stages of grief so that you are aware of where you are on your unique healing journey.

Now, let's explore each of these stages, which include my interpretation for further exploration.

Shock

Shortly after experiencing a loss, we often experience shock. Shock is most commonly associated with the news of one's sudden death, but not in all cases.

In my experience, the shock is a natural response to loss, and often following in its path is a period of disbelief.

When experiencing shock, symptoms will vary. The most common is the inability to eat or drink, insomnia, temporary immobility or paralysis while trying to process the shock, screaming out loud, body shakes, rapid pulse and breathing, cold, clammy skin, and more.

These symptoms often feel intense on an emotional and physical level that can be draining. But, although they're exhausting, the good news is this stage typically doesn't last for an extended period.

Keep in mind that you can revisit feelings of shock at any point in your healing journey. While it's most common to be the first stage you experience after a loss, it may not be a one-time occurrence.

Remember your healing journey is not linear, and how you grieve is unique to you.

Denial

Denial is often associated with the next stage you experience after the shock from a loss. While I can agree to a certain extent, I know it's not the case for everyone and realize it may not be applicable for you too.

When in the denial stage, it's a period of coping and survival. The goal is to get through the day while still mourning the loss. In my experience, the days were often a blur. Living can even feel pointless or daunting too. However, even when there is doubt, there is grace.

This stage doesn't particularly have symptoms but more so actions to be mindful about, such as avoiding the topic of the loss, acting as if the event never occurred, not facing the facts, unwillingness to accept reality, and more.

It's important to note that denial is a healthy response to allow your mind the mental space to unconsciously absorb the information at a pace that won't send you into a downward psychological spiral. However, when and if this should happen, the denial stage can become unhealthy, and I recommend professional support.

Bargaining

The bargaining stage is when we try to understand the situation within their mind and review how we could have done things differently or better to avoid the loss. It's a stage full of helplessness, vulnerability, and emotional turmoil.

In this stage, we often try to negotiate with loved ones or our higher power, such as God, with a bit of quid pro quo or spiraling downward with the "what ifs" and dwelling on all the things we could have done differently.

All of which is an attempt to repair the broken feeling from the loss. The primary goal is to regain control over a life that feels as though it's crumbling into pieces in an attempt to rebuild its structure and feel stable and whole again.

Guilt

The guilt stage is an interesting one; it's full of emotional and mental turmoil. This stage, too, is about control. However, rather than rebuilding the structure or foundation like denial, this phase is more focused on the need for control and order.

Guilt is an immense feeling in this stage; whether rational or irrational, the mind tries to justify or process the loss. The irrational thoughts arise to find anything to feel guilty about and often make you second guess everything.

This dissecting every detail about the loss is exhausting!

While it's a necessary process for our healing, it's essential to know that staying in this stage for an extended period does not serve your highest good. Honor and experience it, then it's time to move on from it. Do not dwell in this stage.

Anger

Anger is an inevitable feeling when it comes to grief. Feeling anger towards yourself, a loved one, other family members, medical professionals, God, and more or any combination of them at once. You feel as though you are at war with everyone, you against the world!

Anger has no boundaries; therefore, it can wrap its claws around whoever is within its reach with a firm grip! Therefore be mindful of this so you can lessen the wrath anger gives to yourself and towards others.

Again, while all the stages are essential for healing, I feel this is where you reach the point of a possible breakthrough. Allowing yourself to feel the anger and work through the pain you feel from the loss is vital to the healing process. The deeper the pain from the grief, the stronger the anger.

Depression

The depression stage is a dreadful state to be in when it comes to your healing journey. While I wish I could tell you this phase is all rainbows and unicorns, it, naturally, is not. It can be one of the most challenging stages to be in during your healing journey.

While in this stage, the most common signs are feelings of despair, frequent negative thoughts, intense sadness, uncontrollable emotions with both highs and lows, withdrawal from loved ones, increased tiredness, possible insomnia, and more.

Unfortunately, when you reach this stage, do not be alarmed if you stay in this stage for a more extended period. However, with that said, this stage is vital to the growth you will experience for healing; it's also important to acknowledge when you need to seek professional help for severe depression or potential suicidal thoughts.

Acceptance

Acceptance in and of itself is a milestone and often with the notion that everything will be alright by embracing the "new normal" after the loss.

It's important to note that you may never feel 100% alright with the loss you've experienced, and that's perfectly normal, in my opinion. However, you can accept and understand that you will be alright despite the loss, and life must go on.

Transformation

The transformation stage is most likely to occur towards the end of the healing journey once you have accepted the loss. However, know that you will be on a transformative journey throughout the entire healing process.

This continual transformation will come in ebbs and flows that, much like a wave, will carry you onto the shore where it's calm.

Once you're fully in the transformation stage, it is here where you find clarity, a sense of peace, and inner knowing that will lead you to find your purpose.

Purpose

Much like the transformation stage, the purpose stage will be ever-evolving. You may not realize it at the time, but your grief healing journey will eventually lead you to find your purpose or discover a deeper understanding of it. Then, when you look back on your journey and find clarity, you'll soon connect the dots.

When you fully immerse yourself into the purpose stage, you will have newfound meaning to your loss. A renewed sense of hope and passion comes from experiencing deep inner pain and healing from it. When you acknowledge the feeling and accept the call, you spring into action and begin the process of fulfilling that mission.

One of the questions I often receive from my family, friends, clients, and online community is how to know when you're no longer grieving. It is such a great question, and the first time I received it, I needed to reflect on my healing journey and how I healed myself from grief. Ultimately this helped me write my first book, *Healing From Grief*.

Firstly, let me say that if you are experiencing grief resulting from the loss of a loved one, you will likely always miss that person. You miss their presence, laughter, stories, and more, but it doesn't mean that you're still grieving. It's part of the healing journey.

With that said, there is a four-step process to the grieving process:

1. You have worked through the stages of grief.
2. You have healed yourself emotionally, mentally, physically, and spiritually and found peace with what you lost.
3. You have adjusted to your new way of living without what you lost.
4. You are experiencing joy again.

When you have worked through all four steps, you know that you have healed from your grief.

Chapter 3 - Healing Journey

When you experience loss of any kind, you will undoubtedly go through a healing journey. As you work through the stages of grief, feelings associated with trauma, and work towards reclaiming your life by taking control of your healing, there will be various ways to support you.

I want to encourage you to read through the next set of chapters with an open mind and heart. Some of these topics may seem a little "out there" for you, but I'm going to lovingly challenge you to work through your limiting beliefs and see them from a different perspective. Trust me; it'll be worth it and a catalyst for your growth!

What I will be sharing are tried and true methods that I have personally used over the years to assist with my healing and overcoming adversity. In truth, some are more recent than others but are just as important.

Now before I delve deeper into various healing modalities and my framework for developing a warrior mindset, harnessing the power of your inner spiritual warrior, and transforming the deep inner pain, let's discuss trauma.

I did not realize that losing my dad or any other life experiences caused me trauma. It wasn't until I was diagnosed with having signs of PTSD that I began to look closer at my life. My limiting belief associated trauma only with catastrophic events such as a natural disaster or something extremely harmful happened to you, such as abuse. However, that's not true, so I feel it's crucial to discuss this topic in association with your grief, loss, and healing.

There's physical, psychological, and emotional trauma, and in my opinion, spiritual trauma too. Traumatic experiences typically involve a threat to one's life or safety.

Thereby any situation that leaves you feeling overwhelmed, fearful, and isolated can cause trauma. It also doesn't have to involve any physical harm. So, for example, the loss of my dad didn't cause any physical damage; however, it did cause harm to me emotionally and psychologically.

These types of trauma can be caused by singular events, ongoing stress, or even overlooked causes. One-time events could be an injury, violent attack, or an accident that happened unexpectedly or during one's childhood. Ongoing or stressful events could be battling a life-threatening illness, experiencing traumatic events repeatedly, like bullying, domestic abuse, or childhood neglect. Overlooked causes may be the death of a loved one, the ending of a long-term relationship, significant humiliation, natural disaster, or experiencing a deliberate, cruel act.[1]

Moreover, traumatic events can happen to anyone, and if you're already under a significant amount of stress, suffered a series of significant losses, or have been previously traumatized, you're predisposed to experience trauma.

Furthermore, experiencing childhood trauma that is left unresolved can cause severe and long-lasting effects, such as an increased sense of fear and helplessness that carries over into adulthood. I am sure you're aware of possible childhood traumas; therefore, I won't go into further detail on them. Some examples could be neglect or living in an unsafe environment, serious illness, abuse, or intrusive medical procedures, and separation from a parent, to name a few.

When it comes to trauma, it is vital to note that your responses to the trauma are _normal_ reactions to _abnormal_ events, and don't let anyone tell you otherwise. Each of us processes traumatic events differently, as I mentioned previously.[1]

Some signs of emotional or psychological trauma are as follows[1]:

- Anxiety
- Confusion
- Despair
- Extreme sadness
- Fear
- Feelings associated with grief (i.e., shock, denial, guilt, and anger)
- Self-isolation or withdrawal

Untreated emotional and psychological trauma can manifest physical problems such as fatigue, digestive issues, and headaches.

When you have unhealed emotional and psychological trauma, it can cause post-traumatic stress disorder (PTSD) because your nervous system cannot move past the shock and cannot make sense of what happened or how to handle your emotions.[1]

Therefore, as you can see, trauma can very much be linked to feelings of grief associated with varying forms of loss. However, as a friendly reminder, not all loss is traumatic, but a traumatic event often triggers feelings of loss.

With all of that said, recognize that you may have trauma that requires healing. The healing methods you are about to work through can support and even heal your trauma, but I, of course, advise that you work with a trauma-informed medical professional should you need that type of support. The critical thing to remember is to advocate for yourself and do what you feel is best for your overall well-being. There is absolutely no shame in getting professional help, and I am an advocate for it!

Lastly, I want to share with you a quote that has a beautiful reminder about your healing journey. Pema Chodron said, "*Healing comes from letting there be room for all of this to happen: room for grief, for relief, for misery, for joy.*"

Chapter 4 - Developing a Warrior Mindset

After identifying and committing to your healing journey, the first step in my framework is to develop a warrior mindset.

Before discussing the intricacies of developing a warrior mindset, we must first talk about mindset and its two types.

Mindset

What is mindset?

Your mindset is a set of beliefs and thought patterns that shape how you make sense of yourself and the world around you, influencing how you think, feel, and behave in any given situation.

According to Carol Dweck, an American psychologist known for her work on mindset, there are two types of mindset: fixed and growth.

If you have a fixed mindset, you may likely believe that your talent and intelligence solely lead you to be successful and that no effort is required. You may also believe that your abilities are fixed traits and can't be changed.

If you have a growth mindset, you may believe that increasing your intelligence or becoming more talented is possible with dedication and practice. You likely also believe that your talents and abilities can develop over time through persistence and your efforts.

Let's briefly explore some examples between the two mindset types.

Fixed Mindset

- Either I am good at it, or I'm not.
- I'm too old to change my habits now.
- I can't change who I am, this is how I was born.
- If I have to work hard for it, then it's not meant for me.
- If I don't try, then I won't fail.

Growth Mindset

- I can learn to do anything I desire.
- I can take small steps to change my habits no matter my age.
- I'm continually evolving and a work in progress.
- Challenging myself allows me to experience growth.
- I only fail if I don't dare to try.

As you can see from the above examples, between the two, one type of mindset can be limiting, and the other offers expansion for personal growth.

The truth is, your mindset plays a critical role in how you cope with adversities in your life. When facing adversity, someone with a growth mindset is more likely to persevere in the face of challenges or setbacks as they view it as an opportunity to learn and grow. On the other hand, those with a fixed mindset are more apt to throw in the towel and give up in the face of challenging circumstances and adversity.

When moving beyond a fixed mindset, you can do a few different things and incorporate them into a daily practice for strengthening your mindset muscle. Let's review some of the methods:

Mindfulness

Practicing mindfulness with the internal and external dialogue will help you change the way you think and speak over time and raise your energetic vibration. Be mindful of your thoughts and words and flip the switch by replacing negative thoughts or words with positive ones. Speak love into your life and incorporate the "yet mentality." Integrating this word into your vocabulary signals to your brain that you can overcome anything.

Positive Statements

Affirmations, mantras, or powerful "I am" statements can dramatically shift your mindset, in my professional opinion. They can influence your subconscious mind to access new beliefs, thought patterns, and motivate you when the going gets tough. Additionally, they work hand-in-hand with mindfulness and incorporating more positivity in your life and establishing a growth mindset.

Authenticity

Stand in your truth and step into your authentic self. Remove the veil and stop pretending to be someone who you are not. Ultimately, this disrespects who you are at your core and diminishes what you have to offer others. Being authentic to yourself often takes deep inner work, but it's worth it!

Celebration

See the progress you have made over time and celebrate the milestones, no matter how small they may be. Embrace the journey, the lessons, and appreciate the opportunities for growth presenting themselves to you. You are transforming internally, which will offer an external reward for you!

Challenges

Have the courage to step out of your comfort zone and try new things. Yes, it can be scary to do so, but you are working through your fear and building resistance. Challenges won't seem insurmountable anymore, and when you face adversity, your body's response to them will be different.

Now that you know the difference between a fixed and growth mindset, let's explore what it means to have mental toughness.

Mental Toughness

What is mental toughness?

Mental toughness is the tenacity and persistence to keep going when we face adversity. When we are mentally tough, it involves our reaction to stress, our response to emotions, our resiliency, and our grit.[1]

Here are some thought-provoking questions to consider when facing adversity:

- Do you crumble when the stress gets to be too much, or do you persist despite it?
- Do you succumb to your emotions, or do you work through them?
- Do you stay in the victim mentality and blame others, or do you accept responsibility?
- Do you give up or push harder when things become too challenging?

Others often see grit being the same as mental toughness; however, while they're similar, they're not the same.

Damon Zahariades, the author of _The Mental Toughness Handbook: A Step-by-Step Guide to Facing Life's Challenges, Managing Negative Emotions, and Overcoming Adversity with Courage and Poise_, states that "_Grit is an attribute that defines our inclination to persevere in adverse circumstances. Mental toughness is a state of mind. It defines our attitudinal durability in such circumstances. It describes our general outlook._"[1]

In short, grit is a vital component of mental toughness because it helps us regulate our responses to negative emotions. Damon believes that it is impossible to be mentally tough and not possess a healthy amount of grit. I would have to agree with him.

He also includes ten benefits for becoming mentally tough in his book, and I feel they're essential to include and align with my ideals when it comes to developing a warrior mindset. Here are his ten benefits[1]:

1. Greater resistance to negative emotions
2. Improved performance
3. Confidence that circumstances will improve
4. Greater ability to manage stress
5. Less susceptibility to self-doubt
6. Greater clarity regarding your intentions and purpose
7. Fearlessness
8. Ability to accept (and learn from) failure
9. Greater ability to delay gratification
10. Willingness to let things go

When it comes to mental toughness, some people are naturally born with more toughness. Thankfully, we can build upon strengthening the inner grit and resilience we have to face adversity. There are some common traits that mentally tough people possess, and I feel we must address those as well.

What are the traits of a mentally tough person?

Here are characteristics of a mentally tough person in no particular order of importance:

1. Ability to distance themselves from things outside of their control and influence
2. Flexibility when dealing with unexpected changes, situations, or events

3. Hope, faith, and belief in oneself and a higher power that they can and will persevere despite the odds
4. Strong intuition and self-awareness to guide yourself without letting your ego take control
5. Adaptability to unforeseen events and willingness to face uncertain circumstances
6. Inner strength to endure pain but still persevere through challenging times
7. Emotional maturity to manage negative emotions that arise from setbacks and disappointments
8. Growth mindset to stay positive despite the adverse circumstances
9. Lack of a victim mentality and self-pity when facing challenging events or situations
10. Self-discipline to set goals and take action no matter how difficult it may be
11. Resiliency to persevere despite setbacks and disappointments
12. Commitment to follow through on what you plan to do

I encourage you to read through the list of characteristics once more and note how many apply to you. You don't need all ten characteristics to be a master of mental toughness, but if you have seven or more, you're in great shape!

Next, we need to discuss a warrior mindset and how it will benefit your healing journey.

Warrior Mindset

What is a warrior mindset?

My definition of a warrior mindset is the mental toughness one needs to overcome mental, emotional, physical, and spiritual challenges and adversities by finding their inner strength to triumph in victory.

Another excellent definition is by Richard Machowicz, a former Navy Seal and the author of _Unleash the Warrior Within: Develop the Focus, Discipline, Confidence, and Courage You Need to Achieve Unlimited Goals_, says, _"Being a warrior is not about the act of fighting. It's about being so prepared to face a challenge and believing so strongly in the cause you are fighting for that you refuse to quit."_

Developing and maintaining a warrior mindset has several benefits. In short, it'll transform your life emotionally, mentally, physically, and spiritually!

Some of the benefits are as follows:

- You won't give up when the going gets tough.
- You will achieve your goals.
- You will be happier and live a healthier life.
- You will feel and be more accomplished.
- You will see an increase in confidence.
- You will experience empowerment.
- You will be open to taking risks.
- You will get out of your comfort zone.
- You will notice a spark in your creativity.
- You have a growth mindset.
- You will experience an increase in positivity.
- You will overcome the adversities in your life

Keep in mind that developing a warrior mindset won't happen overnight. Like with building any muscle, it takes commitment, dedication, and consistency. Therefore, let's briefly discuss some *simple* but powerful ways to find your inner warrior that are in no particular order of importance.

- Avoid taking things personally; not everything is about you.
- Ditch the fear, judgment, and shame you feel about your past, present, or future.
- Take control of your life and stand in your personal and spiritual power.
- Practice mindfulness and self-awareness daily.
- Eliminate failure from your vocabulary; it's a life lesson.
- Accept that setbacks are merely an opportunity for growth.
- View every setback as a lesson for a comeback.
- Remove anything in your life that doesn't serve your highest and greater good.
- Remove the toxicity in your life like people, things, tasks, etc.
- Find the blessing in disguise in everything, literally.
- Ditch the victimhood mentality and take ownership of your actions.
- Surround yourself with like-minded people who uplift you and challenge you often.
- Establish a daily routine and discipline yourself.
- Be proactive, not reactive to adverse situations.
- Gain mental clarity and focus through meditation mindfulness practices.
- Get out of your comfort zone regularly.
- Fuel and train your brain daily by reading, listening to, watching videos, taking a course, etc.
- Limit distractions and be present.
- Believe in yourself wholeheartedly.
- Take action when it intuitively feels aligned and is for your highest good.
- Discover and know what unlocks your inner warrior (aka "beast mode")
- Commit to your vision and mission as if your life depends on it.

Additionally, when developing or enhancing your warrior mindset, it's essential also to consider neuro-linguistic programming (NLP). NLP works as a powerful igniter to support a growth mindset. Let's discuss this further.

Neuro-Linguistic Programming (NLP)

What is NLP?

John Grinder, a linguist, and Richard Bandler, an information scientist and mathematician, are the primary founders that developed neuro-linguistic programming in the 1970s in California and gained popularity when they began marketing the approach as a tool for people to learn how others achieve success.[2]

NLP is a psychological approach to change someone's thoughts and behaviors to help achieve desired outcomes for them and uses perceptual, behavioral, and communication techniques to assist in the desired change.

There are numerous benefits to utilizing NLP. As a certified NLP Practitioner, I could share droves of information with you, but let's zero in specifically on how it helps with grief and loss for the brevity and sake of time.

For starters, the unconscious mind stores most trauma. As mentioned previously, trauma often includes a feeling of loss; however, not all loss is traumatic, but grief can be an experience of loss. Therefore, to reiterate my point, when you experience grief and loss, it is possible also to experience trauma. Now, if you don't know if you have undiagnosed trauma, you can still utilize NLP for your healing with grief and loss.

When we experience trauma, it's the lighter fluid adding fuel to the fire behind negative or toxic thoughts, behaviors, and actions in our lives. Each person processes their thoughts, emotions, feelings, and trauma differently.

NLP is a powerful tool to utilize as it helps each person have a unique experience in transforming their life.

Since we store our trauma in our unconscious mind, we are unaware of how it impacts our daily lives. The goal to heal the trauma that's associated with grief and loss is to stop the triggers. NLP helps us work through the emotions that the trauma evokes so that we no longer hold onto it, allowing the trauma to control the decisions we make or actions we take in life.

How do we leverage NLP to support our healing? Truthfully, I recommend working with a professional who works with neuro-linguistic programming, such as a certified practitioner or a psychotherapist.

Are there safe exercises you can do yourself? Yes, absolutely, but working with a professional who can help you process the emotions and progress through the healing journey is ideal and important since grief, loss, and trauma are all sensitive topics. Please use your judgment and proceed with caution.

There is future pacing, visualization, pattern interrupt, belief change, and anchoring when it comes to NLP techniques, to name a few.

For now, I want to focus on future pacing. Future pacing allows a person to see, hear, feel, and experience what they would like to change or, in other words, manifest in their life. For the record, I'm using the term manifest loosely because we also need to be realistic with this exercise.

Through the process of experiencing what one desires, they imprint what they want in their subconscious mind. If you don't know, the subconscious mind is the part of the brain responsible for the reactions and automatic actions we take as we become aware of or when we think about them. Therefore, you can see why NLP and future pacing exercise can be a powerful tool to use in changing your thoughts and behaviors.

Here is an NLP exercise that I recommend you try to assist with your healing:

Think about the situation in which you experienced grief and loss and how it made you feel. Using your senses, determine how you would like to face the same or similar situation or when triggered in the future.

What would you see, hear, feel, smell, taste?
Who would be with you?
What would you be doing?
Where would you be?

Next, visualize in your mind's eye this scenario to help anchor it into your subconscious mind.

When done, revisit the experience and note how you feel about it now after doing the future pacing exercise. Notice the differences and make a note of the changes in a journal.

Moving on, let's talk about the importance of creating a mindset routine and examples of what to include in this daily practice.

Daily Mindset Routine

Creating a daily mindset practice has several benefits, and some of them are:

- Reduces stress
- Alleviates tension
- Reduces anxiety and depression symptoms
- Boosts confidence and self-esteem
- Increases feelings of peacefulness, calmness, and relaxation
- Increases creativity
- Boosts and shifts energy.

- Promotes feelings of happiness and joy
- Increases productivity
- Develops healthy habits

When establishing a new routine, consistency is the key to success. Therefore, we want to create a daily practice that is easy for us to stick to and challenges us. Of course, you can always add to it in the future; however, I recommend choosing 3-5 activities that you will consistently complete daily for at least 30 days.

Some options to consider are as follows:

- Affirmations or mantras
- Bible study
- Dancing
- Exercise or yoga
- Gratitude practice
- Journal writing
- Mindful meditation
- Perform a power pose (i.e., Superwoman)
- Read a book
- Tarot, oracle, or other card readings
- Visualization

The choice is yours, have fun with it!

I also recommend that you incorporate an activity that allows you to be in your creative flow if you're a creative person. Whether that be creating a piece of art, singing, scrapbooking, or whatever else your heart desires, do it.

Last but not least, to give you an idea of how to create a daily mindset practice, let me share with you mine to help you get started.

My daily mindset routine is simple. I like to mix it up sometimes by adding in one or two additional tasks for variety since I get bored quickly, but the basic daily practice is the same.

1. Mindful meditation
2. Intuitive card reading
3. Journal Writing
4. Exercise
5. Nutrition

I take 10-15 minutes for mindful meditation. There are times I feel I need a guided meditation, other times soft relaxing music or binaural beats, and other times I sit in the quietness of my home and get into my meditative zone. During my meditation, it's also the time I pray and visualize in my mind's eye my goals and desires and anchor them into my subconscious mind.

Next, I pull a card or two, and the kind of cards vary too. I tune into my intuition and determine which of my card decks are *speaking* to me. Sometimes it'll be a tarot deck; other times, it's oracle cards, an affirmation card deck, or angel cards. I go with the flow but stick to pulling at least one card daily.

From there, I journal. I write down any divine downloads that came through during my meditation. I journal about the card(s) I pulled and the intuitive messages I receive from looking at them. I write down and say out loud at least three things I am grateful for, and they cannot be something I used previously. I choose at least three affirmations or mantras to reflect upon for the day and say them out loud as well. I log any thoughts, feelings, or emotions that are bothering me to release and let go. Lastly, I'll work through some shadow work for inner healing, which I will be discussing in more detail in the next chapter.

I also strive to get at least 30-minutes of exercise daily. Unfortunately, I cannot always do this right away in the morning, so I am flexible to fit it in throughout my day. The point is that I'm committed to completing this task, even if that means I'm doing laps throughout my house late at night.

The last thing I work into my daily practice, especially in the morning, is taking my supplements to ensure my body receives the proper nutrients it needs to perform at its optimum best. With underlying health conditions, I need to be mindful of the supplements my body needs to reduce symptoms and be aware of my limitations regarding food.

There's a saying that "Food is Medicine," and I 100% believe in that!

The truth is, your body cannot survive without the proper nutrients. Eating a well-balanced diet can give your body the fuel it needs to thrive. Therefore, in addition to supplements, I review or plan my meals for the day to ensure I am eating a balanced diet.

Eating a balanced diet means you're eating the right balance between food groups. The diet should be low in fat, sugar, and salt and high in fiber. It would be best if you also considered eating the color of the rainbow with fresh fruits and vegetables.

A well-balanced diet is optimal for most people's health. I, however, decided to not only change my "diet" but to change my lifestyle by replacing the foods I used to with healthy alternatives. Here is a quick recap of the changes I made to my healthy lifestyle plan:

- Eliminated gluten
- Eliminated beef and pork
- Eliminated the C.R.A.P. (carbonated beverages, refined sugar, artificial colors and sweeteners, and processed foods)
- Decreased dairy
- Decreased carbohydrates

- Increased consumption of fresh fruits and vegetables
- Increased consumption of seafood, chicken, and turkey
- Increased water intake

While I wish I could say I am perfect and follow this 100%, I don't. I'm human, and I show myself some grace but with discipline. I found that depriving myself of the foods I enjoy only made me crave them more, and I would sabotage my diet. Pointless in the grand scheme of things. It's all about mindful eating and eating in moderation.

Furthermore, one of the tasks I often add-in is energy healing. I'll be honest and say that I don't do energy clearing daily on myself. However, when I feel myself being off-kilter, I'll perform a healing session on myself to clear away any stagnant energy, remove energetic blockages, balance out my system, or what's better known as chakras.

If you're not familiar with energy healing and chakras, don't worry, as I will dive into those topics in a forthcoming chapter.

All right, that's a wrap! Take a look at the Action Step below to implement what you learned in this chapter and when done; we'll move onto discussing shadow work.

***

Action Step: Take 10-15 minutes to outline and create a daily mindset routine that will strengthen your mindset muscle and assist you in developing a warrior mindset. I recommend you review my daily mindset routine and the information I provided to assist you in creating one for success.

Chapter 5 - Identifying the Shadow

The next and second step in my framework is learning to identify the shadow, your darkness, to your light.

To start, I must dispel any notion that it is "woo-woo," mystical, or evil in nature because it's not. Lord, I swear I have seen and heard it all over the years. Yes, this methodology can be used for spiritual work and often is; however, there's more to it than that!

Unfortunately, other so-called leaders in the industry have "glorified" its use to make it appear as something it is not, and it can often get a bad reputation because of it. For example, I have seen people who identify as Christian label it as demonic or the works of the Antichrist. Honestly, it's a shame and why I feel it's important to address the facts.

What is shadow work?

The term 'Shadow Work' was initially given and explored by Carl Jung, psychiatrist, and psychoanalyst. It is a widely used term and philosophy in the field of psychology.

The shadow refers to the parts of us that we may try to hide or deny, and we keep them in the dark or the "shadows." It's aspects of our personality that we often view as shameful, unacceptable, ugly, and the like.

Lonerwolf states, *"Your shadow is the place within you that contains all of your secrets, repressed feelings, primitive impulses, and parts deemed unacceptable, shameful, sinful, or even evil."*[1]

For me, shadow work has been part of my healing journey for as long as I can remember; I didn't know it had a formal name for it and learned more about it over the years. I have always been intrigued by psychology, so it is no surprise that receiving a certification to be a Shadow Work Practitioner became part of my professional credentials.

I want to share a concept of shadow work with you that I feel would help take a complex ideology and simply it further. No doubt, you have likely seen the movie, Peter Pan. If you recall, Peter Pan had a mischievous shadow with a unique personality. At times, it often frustrated Peter, and it was also kind and loving, like a motherly figure.

At the beginning of the movie, he loses his shadow when the dog, Nana, pulls on Peter's shadow as he is trying to escape from spying on the nursery. This experience forces Peter to go back to the nursery to look for his shadow. He knows he needs it as it is part of him, his identity. Without it, he feels lost.

As with Peter, you cannot deny or escape your shadow. It is very much a part of your being, your identity, and when you accept the darker aspects of you, your shadow, you can step more fully into the light.

The moral of the story is that you cannot escape an experience that could help you understand your true self at its core. It's an opportunity to accept the darker parts of yourself, embrace your journey, and experience growth.

Carl Jung said, *"Until you make the unconscious conscious, it will direct your life and you will call it fate."* Interesting quote, isn't it? This is why shadow work is a powerful tool to utilize in your healing to bring what is in the dark, the subconscious, to the light in the conscious.

As mentioned in the previous chapter, I often perform some shadow work while doing my daily journal writing; however, a more immersive experience is necessary for deep inner healing.

When I utilize shadow work with my journal writing, it's often to address something that has triggered me. For example, a common trigger for my entrepreneurial clients is seeing a colleague post online that they're celebrating a $100k cash month as a new coach while they're barely making ends meet. By identifying the trigger, working through the feelings and emotions, they can heal and move forward. Essentially, it's a quick fix in this circumstance.

However, when dealing with grief and loss and possible trauma, deep inner healing is necessary and requires a more immersive process. Utilizing shadow work to delve deeper into those wounds to help them heal is essential. I'll forewarn you; shadow work can be brutal! It will trigger you, drudge things up from the past, open old wounds, and more, but it is worth it.

Unfortunately, when it comes to grief and loss, society prefers to avoid the topic, which is quite sad when you think about it. It's a natural part of life, and there shouldn't be such a stigma around it. Therefore, if you feel alone, know that you are not, and this exercise can help you move beyond the pain you're experiencing.

When going through the grieving process after a loss, no matter the type of loss, we often experience grief itself, sadness, despair, loneliness, confusion, anger, and pain, to name a few. Moreover, this stuck energy from unprocessed feelings and emotions forms limiting beliefs and patterns and is stored in our psyche and wreaks havoc on our bodies when healing doesn't occur for the deep internal pain.

You can see the importance of shadow work, especially if experiencing grief and loss. Therefore, let's delve deeper into this topic.

The benefits of shadow work are:

- Freedom from our ingrained programming and conditioning
- Enhancing our capacity for healthy and intimate relationships
- An awakened sense of wholeness, alignment, and grounding

- Shifted perspective on old wounds
- Creates space for inner healing on various levels (ie, emotionally, mentally, psychologically and spiritually)
- Increases energy and improves our vitality
- A deepened sense of empathy and compassion for others

When it comes to working with your shadow and using it to heal your inner pain associated with grief and loss, there's a simple five-step exercise you can follow.

Step 1: Identify an aspect of your shadow.
Step 2: Write down and reflect on the shadow aspect you identified.
Step 3: Recall a previous experience with the identified aspect of your shadow.
Step 4: Heal the inner child.
Step 5: Integrate the shadow aspect into your life.

Please note that you can do this five-step process outside of your grief and loss healing journey as well. The process will be the same no matter what aspects of the shadow you want to identify.

To give you a general idea of utilizing shadow work, let's do the five-step exercise together for a long-term relationship ending due to infidelity. I like to ask questions and write them in a journal to organize my thoughts. I recommend you do the same.

Step 1: Identify an aspect of your shadow.

Q - What is something that I judge in myself or other people that is triggering me? Infidelity

Step 2: Write down and reflect on the shadow aspect you identified.

Q - Why am I judging myself or others about infidelity? I want a loving relationship where each person is 100% committed and faithful.

Step 3: Recall a previous experience with the identified aspect of your shadow.

Q - Why does this aspect of my shadow profoundly impact me? I am triggered and feel jealous when I see a loving couple or hear how good their marriage is because it reminds me of my failed marriage and my spouse breaking my trust. It makes me angry at myself, my spouse, and men altogether. I feel there is something wrong with me, that I wasn't or am not good enough. Maybe not attractive enough. I feel broken, like trash. I don't see how I could trust again in a relationship, and I'm worried it'll happen again if I let my guard down and date in the future. I want a loving and healthy relationship with someone committed, but I fear I will only continue to attract cheaters.

Step 4: Heal the inner child.

Q - What does my inner child need to hear right now? You are loved. There is nothing wrong with you, don't let anyone else tell you or make you feel differently. You're kind, beautiful, and any person would be lucky to have you in their life.

Step 5: Integrate the shadow aspect into your life.

Q - What affirmations or changes in my life can I make to help integrate the shadow into my life? Some affirmations I can say are: I am enough. I am worthy of a loving and committed relationship. I am kind and beautiful. I only attract loving committed partners into my life.

I hope this fictitious example helps give you a general idea of shadow work and how you can utilize it in your life. Of course, I recommend that you work with a Shadow Work Practitioner, like myself, or a psychotherapist when digging deep into your emotional trauma. Inevitably, things will pop up that you may not know how to handle or process.

Review the Action Step below, and then in our next chapter, we will explore various alternative and holistic healing methods to assist you in your healing journey.

***

Action Step: When ready, get a notebook and pen and complete the five-step exercise. Focus on one emotional trigger and delve deeper into it. Continue to keep asking yourself questions to help you get to the real root of the trigger and the shadow part of yourself you're keeping suppressed.

Chapter 6 - Utilizing Alternative & Holistic Healing Methods

The third step to my transforming inner pain framework is using alternative and holistic healing to support grief and loss.

This chapter will discuss various alternative and holistic healing therapies, methods, and modalities that can assist you with your grief and loss. I will specifically cover various types of energy healing modalities, aromatherapy, chromotherapy, Emotional Freedom Technique (EFT), nutrition, and sound therapy.

To kick things off, let's first explore energy healing. It will tie into several of the alternative and holistic healing therapies, methods, and modalities covered in this chapter.

Energy Healing

Energy healing has become one of my absolute favorite alternative and holistic methods for healing from grief and loss and various other issues. I did not express much interest in this modality until I experienced my dad's passing and embarked on my healing journey.

Therefore, in full transparency, it is not a healing modality I practiced in my youth or young adult life for supporting me through the feelings of grief and loss after facing several adversities in my life, except for acupuncture when it was used to help with my infertility. However, I practice various healing modalities currently and will share with you the ones that have been a catalyst to my healing since my dad's transition.

The topic of energy healing is quite broad. While I would love to delve deeper into this topic, I will keep it simplified as I will assume this topic is likely new to you. Therefore, I will provide you with a general overview of energy healing to ensure you have a basic understanding of it. I'll also provide you with a few simple energy healing modalities that you can implement yourself in the comforts of your home.

Lastly, I'll discuss a handful of energy healing therapies that I love, which require specific training, and it's my recommendation that a certified holistic healing practitioner, like myself, conducts them on you or your loved ones.

To start, what is energy healing?

Energy healing therapy aims to create a state of peace, balance, optimum health and to remove any energy blockages or imbalances that lead to ailments that impact your mind, body, soul, and spirit. This form of holistic healing works on every level of your life - emotionally, mentally, physically, and spiritually.

Skeptics around the world continually ask if energy healing works. The short answer is yes! There are over sixty hospitals worldwide that offer energy healing as part of their alternative treatment options. A study done in 2013 found that 10 minutes of energy healing was as effective as physical therapy in improving the range of motion in people with mobility problems.[1]

Isn't that incredible?

Moreover, there are numerous benefits for receiving energy healing therapy, some of the reported benefits are as follows:

- Generates overall peace and happiness
- Aids in releasing harmful addictions and habits
- Relaxes the mind and body
- Establishes calmness and balance
- Improves mental clarity and concentration
- Releases negative emotions and thoughts
- Relieves stress, anxiety, and depression
- Dissolves energy blockages
- Improves increases energy
- Strengthens self-esteem and confidence
- Clears away built-up toxins
- Reduces fatigue and improves sleep
- Restores your health and strengthens the immune system
- Eases stiffness, pain, tension, and discomfort
- Increases injury recovery rate
- Balances the heart rate, blood pressure, and cortisol
- Assists in reducing or eliminating a chronic problem
- Promotes better digestion

Furthermore, there are a variety of different energy healing modalities. Some of them include Reiki, angelic healing, crystal healing, Emotional Freedom Technique® (EFT), and other holistic methods include acupuncture, acupressure, to name a few.

Next, it is essential to understand how grief impacts your body, its chakras, and why energy healing is a powerful therapy to use not only when you're grieving but also regularly to maintain optimal well-being.

There are four components of grief: emotional, mental, physical, and spiritual. Historically, as children, we often learn to use our heads to deal or cope with sorrow rather than our hearts. Unfortunately, this isn't helpful when experiencing grief because your heart is the most impacted by a loss.

Emotional

When we look at the emotional component of grief, it's necessary to understand how your heart reacts to the pain. Since grief is a very emotional reaction to loss, it impacts the heart the most. Emotions are the foundation to support your grief and allow others to try and understand what you are going through. It may become challenging to cope effectively and healthily with your grief by not accepting these emotions or feelings.

Mental

The mental component of grief is how your mind responds and reacts to the loss. When we consider the mental aspect of a loss, we need to consider the psychological impacts. Often this can be seen as mood disorders, such as anxiety or depression, or as shock and guilt, to name a few. The mental component is linked to emotions and can cause inner turmoil and a domino effect of physical ailments if not addressed quickly or adequately.

Physical

As we look at the physical component of grief, it's necessary to understand that the emotional and mental components of the pain play a part in how your body reacts to the loss. All of this is part of the domino effect I mentioned previously. The body reacts to grief often by crying and emitting stress hormones that weaken the immune system. The weakened immune system hurts the physical body's ability to resist disease, and as a result, there is susceptibility to illnesses. Some illnesses could include headaches, loss of appetite, weight gain, increased blood pressure, physical pain, and more. By not addressing the physical aspects of grief, your body may not have the energy and endurance to move through the stages of grief healthily.

Spiritual

The spiritual component of grief impacts how the spiritual side of you and your beliefs react to the loss. These impacts could lead to questioning your religious beliefs or having negative and positive thoughts about God, your religion, the situation you're experiencing, and more. It can also trigger you to question things about your life, its purpose, or the meaning of life in general. By not addressing and understanding how your grief impacts your spirit and soul, you cannot know how it affects your spiritual beliefs, which may cause you to miss a crucial aspect of your healing journey.

As you can see, each component builds upon the other and is a domino effect in terms of your whole health and well-being, which is why it's essential to treat yourself whole-istically. By treating only one component of grief, you are essentially throwing a bandaid on it and hoping it'll heal the problem. The fact of the matter is, it won't. You will not see progress with your healing journey if you don't address the root of the problem and how it impacts you emotionally, mentally, physically, and spiritually.

Now that you understand how grief can impact your overall well-being, it's necessary to learn how energy healing supports your healing journey. For starters, thinking in terms of quantum physics, we know that atoms are spinning and vibrating vortices of energy. Since everything consists of atoms, everything also has energy. Therefore, we, too, are components of energy, frequency, and vibration.

There are several forms of energy. Some of them include chemical, electromagnetic (light), kinetic (motion), nuclear, thermal, and radiant energies. If we were to use electromagnetic energy as an example, light has different energy colors because of the various wavelengths. Red has the longest and slowest wavelength, whereas violet has the shortest and fastest wavelength.

Interestingly, color plays a vital role in our lives too. They can impact us both negatively and positively as a whole, especially when considering the four components of grief: emotional, mental, physical, and spiritual.

As an example, one person may feel deeper feelings of love when wearing the color red, and another could feel anger. Each person is different, and colors play a unique role in each other's lives and their healing journey.

Furthermore, we must understand and accept that energy is all around us and part of our daily lives. Therefore, when we utilize energy healing to support our feelings of grief and loss, we tap into the energy around us to help us stay balanced and aligned while supporting our healing journey.

Moreover, energy healing therapy can be performed in person or at a distance. However, never without consent unless there are circumstances that prevent them from providing permission to receive healing. Such as if they're a child, medical reasons, or they're nearing their end of life, for example.

Additionally, distance energy healing works because a practitioner can send the healing energy via thought, emotion, and intention to the recipient stretching beyond the limits of time and space. The process sends healing to the recipient, no matter where they are. Energy healing also does not include being touched, adjusted, or manipulated physically. Therefore it is safe.

A healing session is an exchange of energy between the healer and the recipient. It's important to mention that the healer is not playing God or acting as if they are God-like. A healer acts as a conduit for the healing energy from their higher source and the recipient.

When we talk about higher sources, it's crucial to understand whom the practitioner works with for the healing. Let's be fully transparent; some do not operate with the same beliefs as you and can call upon various spirits, energies, or entities for assistance. Please, for your safety, do your research about the practitioner before receiving an energy healing session. I do not wish to cause you any fear but rather to create awareness.

Also, as a side note, if an energy healing practitioner happens to act as though they are God or anything of that nature, they are not practicing with integrity. I recommend you steer clear and find someone else!

As mentioned previously, there are several forms of energy healing available to you. I encourage you to do your research to determine which healing modalities would be a good fit for you and your unique needs.

With that said, I do want to share with you that as a certified energy healing practitioner, I can offer some professional guidance and wisdom to support your decision to receive energy healing.

When performing energy healing services for my clients, I combine several modalities with a Christian focus to pack a powerful punch to the healing session. Those energy healing modalities that I combine are Advanced Angelic and Crystal healing and Usui Reiki. I also include aromatherapy, chromotherapy (color), and sound therapy. As well as utilize my intuition, spiritual gifts, and forms of divination to assist with the healing session.

Furthermore, if we consider energy healing only, for the time being, we want to note that the result is the same - unblock and balance chakras or energy centers. There are seven main chakras throughout our bodies. Chakra means "wheel" as an Indian Sanskrit word. These "wheels" have a circular shape representing a spectrum of colors located along the spine.

Each chakra has a specific color associated with it, along with particular qualities and energies. They must work together for you to feel your best and have optimal health. When the chakras are blocked or unbalanced, the result can lead to several ailments throughout your body.

Let's explore each chakra so you can have a general understanding of how they play a role in your healing journey.

Root Chakra (1st)[2][3]

The root chakra is associated with the element Earth and vibrates with the color red. It's located at the base of the spine and includes the legs, feet, bones, large intestine, teeth, and adrenal glands. The purpose of this chakra is grounding, stability, survival, endurance, passion, courage, and individuality. It corresponds to your physical identity and is also the host to fear when the chakra is not aligned.

When this chakra is out of alignment, some physical manifestations include your body feeling heavy or sluggish, sciatica pain, weight issues, or even constipation. You may also feel mentally scattered, ungrounded, or have a deep attachment to feeling secure, usually due to fear.

Sacral Chakra (2nd)[2][4]

The sacral chakra is associated with the element water and vibrates with the color orange. It's located just above the pubic bone but below your belly button and includes the hips, low back, groins, sexual organs, womb, kidney, bladder, and circulatory system. The purpose of the sacral chakra is movement or flow, desire, pleasure, sexuality, procreation, sensitivity, feelings, confidence, enthusiasm, joy, and your inner child. It corresponds to your emotional identity, and guilt is often a result of the chakra being out of alignment.

When the sacral chakra is out of alignment, some of the ailments you may experience are impotence, bladder, kidney, or uterine trouble, mental issues, and lower back pain. You may also feel over-emotional or numb, careless, or promiscuous, to name a few.

Solar Plexus Chakra (3rd)[2][5]

The solar plexus chakra is associated with the element fire and vibrates with the color yellow. It's located above the belly button but below your heart and includes the upper abdomen, gallbladder, liver, small intestine, stomach, muscles, pancreas, and adrenals. The purpose of this chakra is willpower and ego, assertiveness, laughter or humor, optimism, curiosity, learning, and comprehension. It corresponds to your ego identity, and shame results from the solar plexus being out of alignment.

When the solar plexus is not aligned, you may experience some of the following ailments; ulcers, diabetes, hypoglycemia, digestive issues, or food allergies.

Heart Chakra (4th)[2][6]

The heart chakra is associated with the element air and vibrates with the color green. It's located in the middle of your chest at your heart and includes the heart, ribs, blood, circulatory system, lungs, thymus, breasts, arms, and hands. The purpose of the heart chakra is love, intimacy, balance, relationships, compassion, forgiveness, peace, and harmony, giving without conditions. It corresponds to your social identity, and the demon, the result of an unbalanced chakra, is grief.

When this chakra is not in alignment, some of the ailments you may experience are asthma, respiratory issues, high blood pressure, heart or lung disease. You may also experience codependency, the need to meddle or desire for attention, feel judgemental, or isolate yourself.

Throat Chakra (5th)[2][7]

The throat chakra is associated with the element sound and vibrates with the color blue. It's located at your throat and includes neck, mouth, ears, shoulders, thyroid, parathyroid, trachea, cervical vertebrae, vocal cords, and esophagus. The purpose of the throat chakra is communication, creativity, trust, and wisdom. It corresponds with the creative identity, and its reaction to an unbalanced chakra is lies.

When the throat chakra is out of alignment, some ailments may include thyroid issues, speak loudly or scattered, talk too much, or may even be shy or have difficulty speaking.

Third-Eye Chakra (6th)[2][8]

The third-eye chakra is associated with the element light and vibrates with the color indigo. It's located in the middle of your forehead and includes your eyes, nose, sinuses, pineal gland, pituitary gland, and central nervous system. The purpose of this chakra is intuition, insight, vision, imagination, understanding, fearlessness, release, and memory. It corresponds with the archetypal identity, and the adverse reaction to imbalance is an illusion.

When this chakra is not aligned, some of the ailments may include headaches, poor eyesight, earaches, and nightmares.

Crown Chakra (7th)[2][9]

The crown chakra is associated with the element consciousness and vibrates with the color violet (or white). It's located at the top or crown of your head and includes the head, brain, skin, central nervous system. The purpose of this chakra is spirituality, bliss, wisdom, understanding, awareness, higher self, charisma, awakening, and union with the Divine (your source or a higher power - God). It corresponds with the universal identity, and attachment or ignorance is the casualty of the imbalanced chakra.

When the crown chakra is out of balance, some of the ailments you may experience are migraines, tension headaches, depression, confusion, alienation, boredom, apathy, and inability to learn. You may also feel disconnected from reality and the Divine, be overly concerned with your intellect, be cynical, close-minded, and develop a spiritual addiction.

As mentioned previously, the heart is most impacted by grief. Therefore, the fourth or heart chakra requires the most healing and care when experiencing grief and loss.

Moreover, grief can impact all of the other chakras causing them to become out of balance or be blocked; however, more often than not, the heart chakra needs the most attention, so it is important to remember that when working through your grief and healing.

Unfortunately, grief is an energy-depleting emotion, and it sucks the energy out of you. Your body needs the strength to be healthy and to move beyond grief and loss. Energy can come from eating a balanced diet, getting exercise, being in nature, listening to music, and more.

Much like recharging your cell phone's battery, you need to recharge too. Sadly, if you don't take time to replenish, you will not feel your best and, over time, will begin to feel worse. Your body can only endure so much abuse and neglect, and once it reaches its breaking point, several ailments will follow. It's inevitable when you're putting your body through hell and not caring for it as you should.

When grieving, your entire being is out of balance, and that is why energy healing can support you when experiencing grief and loss. For example, mentally, you may be experiencing anxiety. Emotionally you may feel a sense of shock or anger. Physically you may experience loss of appetite, fatigue, or a feeling of heaviness throughout your body. Spiritually, you may feel lost and alone. All of these are manifestations of the body when your chakras aren't in alignment.

When receiving energy healing, the goal is to improve or maintain the flow of energy within the body, which will activate the healing process. This energy knows precisely where to go to balance chakras and heal the body. There's a well-known philosophy that energy healing will give you what you need, not what you necessarily want.

Additionally, it's crucial to mention that energy healing does not magically take away someone's grief and sadness. It does offer support to deal with the turbulent ups and downs as they move through each of the nine stages of grief. Being calm and collected gives the energetic space to process emotions healthily and heal from the loss.

Are there physical benefits of energy healing to support your grief? Yes, there are! In short, energy healing helps to increase energy, reduce muscle tension, and clear toxins.

Replenishing your energy and balancing your chakras is vital to get through the day without feeling out of alignment. It makes it easier for your body to fight off any illnesses that can prolong your healing journey too.

Furthermore, grief can cause physical pain throughout the body; however, with the support of energy healing, it reduces muscle tension that is wreaking havoc on the body through tensed shoulders, clenched jaw, headaches, and more. As the pressure builds, it can cause worry and anxiety. When relaxed, you can cope and handle your grief and support your body through the healing process.

Lastly, the body continually burns energy to rebuild tissue and replaces older or damaged cells throughout the body. Therefore, the body creates a significant amount of waste (internal toxins) that the body must break down and eliminate. Unfortunately, grief can contribute to the toxins staying within the cells, soft tissue, and muscles of the body, causing it to overwhelm your entire immune system. As a result, the body can't effectively break down and eliminate waste. When these toxins build-up, the body is susceptible to illness. Energy healing can support the body to clear the toxins allowing for optimal health and overall improved well-being.

As you can see, energy healing goes hand in hand with supporting those suffering from grief. The benefits, in my opinion, are invaluable, and I highly recommend energy healing for anyone no matter their age or circumstance because I have felt and experienced its power, and so should you.

Moreover, I recommend having a certified practitioner, like myself, perform the healing session with regard to the following two energy healing modalities. With that said, you can find reputable practitioners on YouTube who offer a general healing session that you could listen to at your leisure; however, it will not be as potent of a healing session as you would have individually with a professional working specifically on you and your issues.

To each is their own, but I would be remiss if I didn't state that I strongly recommend individual healing sessions when needing support for your grief and loss.

Without further ado, let's explore angelic and reiki healing!

Advanced Angelic Healing

When it comes to angelic healing, it is just that, allowing the angels to do the healing. As someone who identifies as a Christian, I was excited about learning how to call upon the angels to utilize their healing power. What I love about this healing modality is, to me, at least, it aligns with my religious beliefs. I also like that you don't have to know anything about the chakras, and if you would like to incorporate crystals, essential oils, or music, it's optional, not required.

As an Advanced Angelic Healing Practitioner, my role is to be a guide to call upon the angels and hold the physical, energetic, and spiritual space for the healing. I won't get into all of the backstory and history of angels and nine celestial choirs right now, but I will share with you that there are several types of angels, and each grouping serves a purpose.

There is a hierarchy for the angels, and the archangels are on the second rung of this hierarchical ladder. We often hear more about angels than any other choir because it is their job, so to speak, to help us. They are the closest to our earthly level.

Additionally, there are various archangels that a practitioner could call upon; however, we have seven that we specifically include in the healing for this particular modality.

Let's discuss each of the archangels and their rule in assisting with this healing modality.

Please keep in mind that each archangel can help you with a multitude of issues within your life, and this is not a fully comprehensive overview outlining every possible way they can support you. Instead, it's a brief overview highlighting a few important details that'll give you a general idea about how this healing modality operates.

Archangel Michael

Archangel Michael is the leader of all the angels and archangels and serves on God's blue ray, or what's known as the ray of protection. He can assist with physical and spiritual protection, including safety from accidents, crime, psychic attacks, demons (yes, they exist!), and more—also, one of the most well-known archangels.

Archangel Jophiel

Archangel Jophiel serves on the yellow ray of illumination and can assist with helping you absorb information. For example, when you're studying or when you need wisdom.

Archangel Chamuel

Archangel Chamuel serves on the pink ray of spiritual love and can help you resolve relationship problems, find a job or career path, or even assist with locating a lost item.

Archangel Gabriel

Archangel Gabriel serves on the white ray of purity and can assist with helping you establish discipline and order within your life, provide guidance, and more. Also, one of the most well-known archangels, especially if you're a Christian, as he told Mary she would give birth to baby Jesus.

Archangel Raphael

Archangel Raphael serves on the green ray of divine healing and can support you with healing your body, mind, soul, and spirit. He's also helpful when you need safety, security, and other physical needs met. Raphael offers healing both traditionally and with alternative medicine and supports individuals and healers in their healing practice. He is also the angel of truth and can provide discernment for spiritual and human truth.

Archangel Uriel

Archangel Uriel serves on the purple ray with gold that's flecked with ruby and known as the ray of peace. Uriel can help you create a peaceful resolution between two parties, calm the chaos of your world, and bring inner peace, tranquility, and the renewal of hope.

Archangel Zadkiel

Archangel Zadkiel serves on the violet ray of forgiveness and can help you if you're struggling with this and also assist with tolerance and diplomacy. He can also help with bringing more joy back into your life.

Now that you know which archangels will assist with the healing and how they can specifically help you, let's explore how this healing operates during a session with a practitioner.

When participating in an angelic healing session, there's no physical manipulation, like seeing a chiropractor, and typically the practitioner doesn't lay their hands on you either. The healing is all done spiritually and energetically and often lasts roughly 45-mins. This healing can be in person or at a distance, like virtually.

The practitioner will create a sacred space for the healing, ask for protection, and quietly or softly whisper to themselves a series of steps calling forth the archangels through a special healing ceremony. You will be lying down in a comfortable position and relaxing.

As mentioned previously, some practitioners will use aromatherapy, sound therapy, and crystals in their sessions. For advanced healing, it is more common to incorporate these options into the session.

Truthfully, energy healing overall requires a significant level of trust in the practitioner. Trust that they are not a scam artist, calling forth any negative spirits, energies, or entities and that they are holding the spiritual and energetic space for your healing.

Additionally, healers can feel the energetic shift when the archangels are present and when energy shifts during a session. They often experience things on an unparalleled level than others by their senses, intuition, and spiritual gifts.

Some clients will feel something during a session, like a noticeable sensation, and others won't feel anything at all. The key thing is to notice what you notice and discuss it with your practitioner.

At the end of the sessions, the practitioner will review anything that came through for them energetically, intuitively or spiritually, discuss energy healing after care protocol, and schedule a follow-up appointment, if needed.

Now that you have a better understanding of angelic healing, we can review reiki healing.

Reiki Healing

Reiki as an energy healing modality. Much like the angelic healing, the setup for a session is similar. You may be lying down or sitting. The use of aromatherapy, crystals, or sound therapy may be used but isn't required. This healing can be in person or at a distance too.

There's no physical manipulation or typically any touching, such as laying the hands on the body. However, in some places globally, laying of hands is a common practice.

Reiki is a Japanese alternative medicine that uses "life force energy" or "universal energy." Founded by Mikao Usui. Reiki comprises two Japanese words - Rei, which means "God's Wisdom or the Higher Power," and Ki which means "life force energy." Therefore, Reiki technically means "spiritually guided life force energy."[10]

Additionally, Reiki is not a religion, nor does it follow one. It is spiritual in nature with the ethical ideals to promote peace and harmony, which is universal across all cultures.

As a certified Usui Master Reiki Practitioner and certified Grief Reiki® Practitioner, I act as the conduit to transfer the healing energy to the client or patient, as do other practitioners. There are specific Japanese symbols used for this healing modality.

An interesting fact is that the practitioner can call upon angels to assist with a reiki session, and it can become an angelic reiki healing session. Along with Usui Reiki, there are other types, such as Holy Fire Reiki. Each follows the same basic concepts but has facets unique in nature, setting themselves apart from each other.

The next group of alternative and holistic healing therapies, methods, and modalities are ones you can do in the comforts of your home or, if you wish, a practitioner. Each of these options will support you with your grief and loss and assist in balancing your energy too. You're welcome to utilize one, a couple, or all if you wish. Trust your intuition and leverage the ones you feel will work the best for you and your given situation.

To start, let's explore how to leverage aromatherapy to support you during significant life-changing situations.

Aromatherapy

Aromatherapy is an excellent way to provide support holistically for your healing. Healthline Media states that *"Aromatherapy is a holistic healing treatment that uses natural plant extracts to promote health and well-being. Sometimes it's called essential oil therapy. Aromatherapy uses aromatic essential oils medicinally to improve the health of the body, mind, and spirit. It enhances both physical and emotional health."*[11]

Aromatherapy dates back to the Ancient Egyptians and Greeks. They have been used for medicinal and religious purposes worldwide too.

Aromatherapy works by activating the smell receptors in your nose that send messages directly to your brain's limbic system. This system affects your emotions, memory, learning, appetite, and sex drive. Therefore, inhaling aromas, such as through essential oils, stimulate different responses throughout your body that provide a positive healing effect.[12]

There are various options for Aromatherapy, and collectively they provide several benefits for supporting the mind, body, soul, and spirit; some of which are as follows:

- Improving focus and mental clarity
- Providing a grounding and balance
- Alleviating pain
- Improve sleep quality
- Reduce symptoms of headaches and migraines
- Boost immunity
- Aiding digestive support
- Reduce stress, anxiety, and support other mood disorders
- Reduce the side effects of chemotherapy treatment
- Kills bacteria, fungus, and viruses
- Promote relaxation

As mentioned, there are various types of aromatherapy. I utilize burning incense, both sticks and raw incense, sage, and palo santo. I also inhale, diffuse, wear or ingest essential oils.

Essential oils are my preferred method of aromatherapy. I became interested in essential oils shortly before my dad was diagnosed with cancer, and once we received his diagnosis, I started using them regularly.

Essential oils are compounds extracted from plants that capture the essence, scent, or flavor. Obtained through mechanical or distillation processes for use in one of three ways: aromatically, topically, or internally.

I must provide a word of caution, do not ingest any essential oils without guidance from a professional who understands essential oils and the body. You will find conflicting information about their use and safety on the Internet; therefore, you must understand the risks.

Let's briefly review how to safely use essential oils, as there is a misconception that they cannot harm you because they are natural. That's completely inaccurate. While they are an excellent way to support you, as with anything, there are things to consider for safety. Here is what we will cover:

- Dosage
- Application
- Dilution
- Storage
- Children
- Health Conditions

Dosage

As with anything that promotes health and wellness, essential oils should be monitored and used with the proper dosage guidelines for adults and children. Essential oils are potent, and only a small amount of the oil is necessary to achieve the result you are looking for. You must be aware of the dosage recommendations to ensure you are safely using the essential oils. The following is the recommended dosage for daily consumption by dōTERRA®.[13]

- Aromatically: No limits

- Topically: For adults, 12-36 drops or for children, 3-12 drops in 24 hours
- Internally: For adults, 12-24 drops or for children, 3-12 drops in 24 hours

Application

As previously mentioned, there are three ways to use essential oils. - aromatically, topically, and internally. Aromatic use is the process of experiencing the aroma of essential oils through the air by inhaling or breathing in oils, often with the use of a diffuser.

Topical use is the process of applying the essential oils to the skin. Places you can topically use essential oils will vary based on the oil, but here are all of the areas on your body to consider.

- Temples or back of neck
- Behind ears
- Over the heart
- Abdomen
- Wrists
- Sole of foot
- Bottom of big toe
- Base of big toe
- Base of pinky toe
- Bottom of pinky toe
- Base of middle toe
- Bottom of middle toe
- Outer arch of foot
- Inner arch of foot
- Heels
- Chest
- Shoulders
- Outside of ears

Internal use is the process of taking the essential oils directly in the mouth, by adding them to food or beverages, or via a capsule and then ingesting them.

It is vital that you have a full understanding of how to use essential oils, their appropriate dosages, risks, and more to ensure you are using them safely for yourself and with your loved ones, including pets!

Dilution

When using your essential oils, it's necessary to follow the guidelines for topical application. Most are safe for use without using a carrier oil, like fractionated coconut oil, but many should be diluted because they are too strong to put directly onto the skin.

As mentioned, the best way to dilute essential oils is with the use of carrier oils. There are a variety of carrier oils available. There is fractionated coconut oil, sweet almond oil, olive oil, argan oil, avocado oil, and grapeseed oil, to name a few. The vital thing to note is the texture and consistency of the oil, and it's odor. I recommend using fractionated coconut oil as a preferred carrier oil, but you're welcome to test out others to determine what will work best for you.

When diluting, you can follow this rule of thumb:

1 tsp of carrier oil + 1 drop of essential oils = 1% dilution

Storage

Storing your essential oils correctly is vital to keep their potency, efficacy, and safety reasons. Make sure the caps are on tight, store in a cool, dry place, and out of the reach of children.

Children

As noted above, it's necessary to keep your essential oils out of the reach of children because they simply don't understand how to safely use them. Children can use essential oils with adult supervision. It's important to mention that children' have more delicate and sensitive skin than adults, so diluting the oils before use is crucial for safe application.

Health Conditions

As you begin to use essential oils, it's necessary to acknowledge and be aware of your personal health conditions. Some medical conditions are not compatible with essential oils. For example, some essential oils are not recommended during pregnancy because they can cause complications.

Yes, it is safe to use essential oils in conjunction with your regular exercise and diet regimen to promote a healthy lifestyle. However, please be your own advocate for your health and consult a medical professional first to address any health concerns.

Now that we have discussed how to safely use essential oils let's explore which oils would be perfect for you to support you in your healing.[14]

Anger

For support with feelings of anger, use any of the following essential oils:

- Bergamot
- Cardamom
- Cedarwood
- Frankincense
- Roman Chamomile
- Spearmint
- Wild Orange
- Ylang Ylang

Anxiety

For support with anxious feelings, use any of the following essential oils:

- Arborvitae
- Bergamot
- Cedarwood
- Clary Sage
- Cypress
- Douglas Fir
- Frankincense
- Geranium
- Grapefruit
- Juniper Berry
- Lavender
- Lemon
- Lime
- Marjoram
- Melissa
- Patchouli
- Roman Chamomile
- Sandalwood
- Vetiver
- Wild Orange
- Wintergreen
- Ylang Ylang

Broken Heart

For support with mending your broken heart, use any of the following essential oils:

- Geranium
- Lime
- Rose
- Spikenard
- Wild Orange
- Ylang Ylang

Emotional Wounds

For support with deep emotional wounds, use any of the following essential oils:

- Eucalyptus
- Frankincense
- Geranium
- Lime
- Myrrh
- Roman chamomile

Denial

For support with feelings of denial or disbelief, use any of the following essential oils:

- Birch
- Black Pepper
- Cinnamon
- Coriander
- Grapefruit
- Juniper Berry

- Marjoram
- Peppermint
- Roman Chamomile
- Sandalwood
- Spearmint
- Thyme

Depression

For support with feelings of sadness or depression, use any of the following essential oils:

- Bergamot
- Douglas Fir
- Frankincense
- Geranium
- Grapefruit
- Juniper Berry
- Lavender
- Lemon

- Lime
- Patchouli
- Peppermint
- Spearmint
- Thyme
- Tangerine
- Wild Orange
- Ylang Ylang

Grief

For support with feelings of grief, use any of the following essential oils:

- Bergamot
- Cedarwood
- Frankincense
- Geranium
- Helichrysum

- Marjoram
- Lavender
- Melissa
- Rose
- Sandalwood

Guilt

For support with feelings of guilt or shame, use any of the following essential oils:

- Bergamot
- Fennel
- Ginger
- Grapefruit
- Lavender
- Myrrh
- Oregano
- Peppermint
- Vetiver
- Ylang Ylang

Hopelessness

For support with feeling hopeless, use any of the following essential oils:

- Lavender
- Lime
- Patchouli
- Vetiver
- Wild Orange
- Ylang Ylang

Shock

For support with feelings of shock use any of the following essential oils:

- Bergamot
- Coriander
- Douglas Fir
- Frankincense
- Geranium
- Helichrysum
- Lavender
- Marjoram
- Melissa
- Peppermint
- Roman Chamomile
- Vetiver
- Wild Orange
- Ylang Ylang

Spiritual

For spiritual connection and support, use any of the following essential oils:

- Cinnamon
- Frankincense
- Juniper Berry
- Myrrh
- Roman Chamomile
- Sandalwood

Trauma

For support with feelings associated with trauma or PTSD, use any of the following essential oils:

- Cedarwood
- Clary Sage
- Cypress
- Frankincense
- Geranium
- Helichrysum
- Jasmine
- Juniper Berry
- Lavender
- Melissa
- Myrrh
- Patchouli
- Roman Chamomile
- Rose
- Sandalwood
- Vetiver
- Wild Orange
- Ylang Ylang

From dōTERRA, I recommend their signature blends Balance®, Console®, Forgive®, and Serenity®. They work beautifully to support you with your grief and loss, and I love that they're blended oils, meaning each one has various oils combined to give you the best results for their use.

A word of caution, though, please do not buy your essential oils from your local drugstore, general merchandise store, or random online retailers. Many oils sold are not high quality, sourced properly, safe for use, and some even contain fillers. There's a saying that not all oils are created equal; that's true! I recommend <u>dōTERRA</u> essential oils as a starting point.

Next, let's discuss chromotherapy and its benefits for use by incorporating color into your life for additional healing support.

Chromotherapy

Chromotherapy, also known as color therapy, is the use of color to heal the physical, mental, and spiritual energy imbalances that often lead to disease.

It's important to note that color therapy is a complementary or alternative medicine therapy and not all medical professionals believe in its healing properties. Therefore, I encourage you to be an advocate for yourself. If you think it works and you are experiencing the benefits of it, continue to use it.

How does chromotherapy work?

Colors all vibrate energetically at different frequencies, and based on that vibration is the color we perceive. Each of the color photons has a separate wavelength and frequency. Interestingly, the body recognizes the wavelengths and frequencies and responds to them. Additionally, each color charges the body's cells a certain way based on the energy frequencies of the color.

The benefits of using color therapy are that it can aid in physical ailments, assist with anti-aging, and has mood-boosting properties, to name a few.

There are numerous ways you can incorporate color into your life. Some are my favorites are as follows:

- Aromatherapy
- Candles
- Clothing
- Crystals
- Food
- Home Decorations
- Meditation
- Visualization

When it comes to using aromatherapy in conjunction with color therapy, you need to consider the color of the essential oil or other types of aromatic proponent you're using.

For example, if we consider essential oils, their origin is typically from a plant (bark, seeds, flowers, etc.). Each has different colors associated with it and a different energetic vibration. As we discussed, vibration healing methods and colors have various wavelengths and frequencies that promote healing.

Therefore, if we want color therapy support with aromatherapy for our grief, we could utilize the color green. We could wear the color green for clothing, eat green foods, and use the rose, bergamot, melissa, or jasmine essential oils that'll offer feelings of love, harmony, and peace.

When we consider the use of candles, we use the color that corresponds to the color therapy we want to utilize. For example, if you are looking for more joy and content, you could consider using an orange candle during a meditation or visualization exercise.

For clothing, it's the same premise. Wear clothing that corresponds to the color therapy healing you need.

Same for food consumption. Eat more foods throughout the day that correspond to the color therapy healing support you need. Looking for more grounding, balance, and stability, eat more red foods, such as red peppers, strawberries, beetroot, radishes, or tomatoes.

For home decor, consider the colors you use on your walls, the decorations in the rooms you spend the most time in, and plants that can pull in the color therapy healing properties you need. For grief, household plants or greenery will help aid in your healing.

When it comes to meditation and visualization, we often use them together simultaneously. Consider visualizing in your mind's eye the color of your choice that corresponds to the color therapy healing you need for support and meditate on it.

I prefer to think of an object to zero in my focus and then visualize that object as my chosen color. For example, if I need a happiness pick-me-up, I could think of something that brings me joy, the color yellow, like a balloon, and imagine myself playing with a yellow balloon in child-like wonder.

Each of these options helps to bring balance to your body, mind, soul, and spirit. Some may offer additional benefits, such as cleansing when using crystals, but the premise is the same when considering how to use each in color therapy. For ease, view the color healing property as the primary benefit, and the rest are additional benefits, more like the sprinkles on a cake.

Get creative in your quest to leverage the powerful benefits of color therapy!

What colors should you utilize to support your grief and loss? When we consider grief and loss, color therapy can stimulate emotions, heal the body and enhance the spirit. Ideally, green, purple (violet), and white are the recommended colors for grief and loss.

Green

Green color therapy enhances the emotions of love, joy, and inner peace and can bring you hope, strength, and serenity, as well as healing.

Purple

Purple or violet color therapy provides mental peace, enhances psychic abilities, aids in spirituality, and supports meditation.

White

White color therapy offers support for self-compassion, inner peace, and protection.

While those colors may help most people with their grief and loss, there are other colors to consider, and it's vital to know how they can benefit your overall healing too. Let's take a quick look; see below.

Blue

Blue color therapy promotes feelings of calmness, peacefulness, and sincerity.

Orange

Orange color therapy aids in emotional expression while increasing social interaction and boldness.

Pink

Pink color therapy provides uplifting energy and emotional support while decreasing aggression.

Red

Red color therapy supports grounding and safety, love, vitality, and courage.

Yellow

Yellow color therapy stimulates happiness, cheerfulness, and positive thinking.

Please also note that each of these colors (and more) provide numerous benefits through color therapy; however, for now, I only covered what's relevant for grief and loss.

Now that you have a basic understanding of color therapy, it's time to discuss crystals!

Crystal Healing

I love crystals and believe they add powerful and natural energy to your healing journey. If crystals are new to you, I ask that you keep an open mind about them. I was skeptical at first, too, but once I experienced their benefits firsthand, I was no longer a skeptic but a believer!

Interestingly, crystals and aromatherapy supported my healing when I weaned off my medications for depression and anxiety. I hope that you'll utilize these magnificent crystals for your inner healing by keeping an open heart and mind.

Healing with crystals is an alternative medical technique used to cure and protect against disease and support other medical ailments. Holistic healing practitioners, like myself, believe crystals act as a conduit for healing by allowing positive healing energy to flow into the body, forcing the negative energy to flow out.

There are several crystals to choose from, and each has its benefits. I don't want to overwhelm you with all the details; therefore, I will share the necessary information with you that you will need to incorporate crystals into your healing journey and to find additional support with your grief, loss, and possible trauma.

To start, how do you use crystals?

Crystal use isn't complicated unless you make it be. You can wear them as jewelry, carry them in your pocket, sleep with them under your pillow, place them around the house or your car, and more.

For the crystals that I am about to share with you, the care for them is simple; therefore, it's time to discuss how to care for and use them properly.

Cleansing your crystals is necessary because they absorb, transform energy and vibrations around them. The beautiful thing about them is that they can turn the negative energy they consume into positive energy. You can cleanse them with water, place them outside under the sun or moon, submerge in salt for a day or two, smudge with sage, or use incense. However, should you choose to purchase other crystals, you will want to research crystal care to ensure you don't inadvertently damage it.

Crystals need charging to gain power, just like a phone battery. Sunlight, moonlight, and higher vibrational crystals such as selenite, quartz, carnelian, amethyst, and kyanite can charge other crystals. These five crystals are also ones that do not need clearing of negative energy, but they are potent enough to clear other crystals from negative energy and recharge them for healing use.

When it comes to using crystals to accompany and support your grief journey, I recommend a few. Each of the crystals I'm about to share with you I have used for my healing journey; therefore, I can attest to their unique healing qualities. Let's explore more about each of the recommended crystals and their specific benefits to support your healing.

Amethyst

Amethyst relieves physical, emotional, and psychological pain or stress. It also eases headaches, releases tension, reduces insomnia, and promotes a better night's rest.[15]

Angelite

Angelite helps you speak your truth, be more compassionate, and accept things you cannot change. It stimulates healing, eases emotional pain, and creates feelings of peace and tranquility. Spiritually this crystal can help you connect with your angels.[15]

Apache Tear

Apache tear is a form of black obsidian and has its name because it's believed to shed tears in times of sorrow. Therefore it offers comfort during grief, provides insight into the cause of distress, relieves grievances, and promotes forgiveness.[15]

Black Onyx

Black onyx provides strength and support during difficult times or confusing situations, especially when dealing with mental, emotional, or physical stress. It alleviates feelings of overwhelm, fear, and worry.[15]

Clear Quartz

Clear quartz is a master healer and can be used for any condition or situation, and is an amplifier stone. Meaning it can amplify the energy of other stones.[15]

Howlite

Howlite is a stone that teaches patience and helps to calm turbulent emotions, assist with releasing trauma, eliminate rage, pain, and stress. It's also an excellent stone for helping with insomnia and meditation because it helps to still the mind.[15]

Kyanite

Kyanite also helps you speak your truth and cut through fear and blockages. It encourages self-expression and communication. Dispels illusion, anger, frustration, and stress as well.[15]

Malachite

Malachite supports your transformation by drawing out deep feelings and psychosomatic causes, breaks unwanted ties, outdated patterns, and taking responsibility for your actions.[15]

Moonstone

Moonstone is known as the "stone of new beginnings," which calms overreactions to situations and emotional triggers. It opens the mind to sudden irrational impulses, serendipity, and synchronicity. It soothes emotional instability and stress and stabilizes the emotions.[15]

Rhodonite

Rhodonite heals emotional shock and panic and clears away emotional wounds or scars from the past, and promotes forgiveness.[15]

Rose Quartz

Rose quartz strengthens your empathy and sensitivity and aids in the acceptance of the change. Emotionally it helps to release emotions and heartache and soothes the internal pain from grief and trauma.[15]

Tiger's Eye

Tiger's eye is helpful for problem-solving and resolving internal conflicts, grounding, and aides in healing mental or personality disorders.[15]

You can find crystals through local businesses such as rock or crystal shops, metaphysical or spiritual stores, or several online retailers. However, be careful about purchasing your stones from random retailers. Some sell fake crystals or grow them in labs. They will not have the same energy properties as those sourced from the Earth.

Lastly, I encourage you to choose a handful of crystals to start with to aid in supporting your healing journey. The five I recommend using are amethyst, apache tear, clear and rose quartz, and tiger's eye to assist you during this difficult time.

Our next healing modality is the emotional freedom technique (EFT); looking forward to delving into this modality with you!

Emotional Freedom Technique (EFT)

I was first introduced to the emotional freedom technique (EFT) with one of my first business coaches back in 2015 as part of a group coaching experience. At first, I was skeptical and genuinely thought it was a bit "out there." We were encouraged to attend, and since I was committed to growing my business under her guidance, I hopped on our group call and proceeded to have an EFT tapping session with a well-known practitioner.

At the start of the session, the practitioner asked us to rate our emotional state on a level of one to ten, with one being the lowest and ten the highest. I focused on my stress and anxiety at the time and gave myself a score of 9.

Life for me was hectic back then. I was a new mom, breastfeeding, and working over forty hours a week with a commute. On the side, I was building my coaching business along with our family real estate investment property business. I was working with multiple coaches, serving my clients, and trying to stay afloat. My stress levels were extremely high!

I figured at this point, what did I have to lose? I scored my stress and anxious feelings high, so if I could get some relief trying something weird, I was down for it. Long story short, after a brief 10-15 minute session, the practitioner asked us to rate ourselves again, and I felt extremely relaxed and scored myself at a two.

I experienced healing in a way I never really thought possible, and it turned my skepticism into being a believer. So much so, later received certifications for EFT and thought field therapy (TFT).

Therefore, I must state for the record that this healing modality is also newer to me and one that I incorporated more after the passing of my dad. While I used it over the last several years, I don't want to give the impression that EFT was a healing modality I used in my younger years to overcome adversity.

With all of that said, let's dive in and explore this topic further!

What is EFT?

According to Healthline, they state, *"Emotional freedom technique (EFT) is an alternative treatment for physical pain and emotional distress. It's also referred to as tapping or psychological acupressure."*[16]

EFT balances our energy system (aka our chakras) and supports us in numerous ways, including offering support with anxiety, stress, trauma, and PTSD. All of which are common when coping with significant life-changing situations and grief associated with loss.

What are the benefits of EFT?

Some of the benefits of EFT are as follows:

- Reduces stress and cortisol levels
- Decreases anxiety symptoms
- Reduces chronic pain
- Improves sleep habits and reduces fatigue
- Reduces psychological trauma and PTSD symptoms
- Decreases depression symptoms
- Reduces frequency and severity of headaches and migraines
- Improves Confidence and self-esteem
- Reduces emotional eating and food cravings
- Improves overall mood
- Reduces triggers associated with fears and phobias
- Aides in balancing the body's energy system

Are there risks?

No, not really. However, as with anything alternative and holistic, you must advocate for yourself because no one knows your body better than you. While I am a complete advocate for this healing modality, I have to state that EFT should best be used as an adjunct therapy if you have a mood disorder or mental illness. As a certified EFT practitioner, it is not ethical for me to encourage EFT if you have a mental illness that requires support from a medical professional.

How does EFT work?

EFT works with the body's energy system. As with traditional Chinese medicine, like acupuncture or acupressure, EFT utilizes the body's energy systems, consisting of circuits that run throughout the body. These energy circuits are known as meridians. I like to think of them as railroad tracks that run throughout our bodies.

You can't see them, nor can they be measured; however, many believe they exist and have potent effects on our bodies. Such as mind and body healing techniques to help direct the flow of energy that promotes overall well-being and balance within the body and promotes physical and emotional healing.

How do you perform EFT?

When it comes to the tapping technique, there are five basic steps to follow. Let's explore them together.

Step 1: Identify the issue or problem
Step 2: Rate the issue or problem
Step 3: Create a statement
Step 4: Perform the tapping sequence
Step 5: Review and re-rate the issue or problem

Now that you know the basic steps, let's discuss each one in further detail.

Identify the Issue or Problem

For this technique to be effective, we must first identify the issue or problem. It is important to choose only one to start, and it'll be your focal point for the session. Doing so will increase the effectiveness of the healing and provide a favorable outcome.

Rate the Issue or Problem

Before we start the session, it is important to rate where you are feeling right now on a scale of one to ten, with one being the lowest and ten being the highest—Determine on the scale where your issue or problem lies. Please write it down for proof, as you will review this number later in the session.

Create a Statement

Once you identify the issue or problem, we need to create a statement to use throughout the tapping sequence. The preferred or traditional method is to use a present tense statement. My recommendation is to use past tense to anchor the thought and shift the language. The present tense states that you are still suffering from the issue or problem. The past tense anchors in the idea that you're not.

The statement you'll use is as follows: *Even though I _____ {insert issue or problem}, I deeply love and accept myself.*

Below is an example for you using anxiety as the targeted problem using both tenses.

1. (Present) Even though I suffer with anxiety, I deeply love and accept myself.
2. (Past) Even though I have suffered from anxiety, I deeply love and accept myself.

Perform the Tapping Sequence

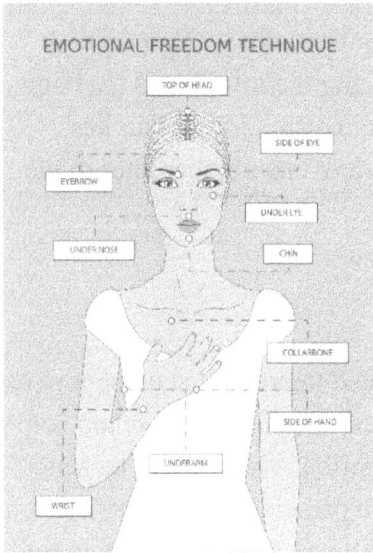

EMOTIONAL FREEDOM TECHNIQUE
TOP OF HEAD
SIDE OF EYE
EYEBROW
UNDER EYE
UNDER NOSE
CHIN
COLLARBONE
SIDE OF HAND
UNDERARM
WRIST

Please refer to the image for the tapping points as a reference point. The tapping points we will utilize in a session are the following:

- Side of hand ("Karate chop")
- Top of head
- Eyebrow
- Side of eye
- Under eye
- Under nose
- Chin
- Collarbone
- Underarm

Begin by tapping the side of the hand while reciting your statement from the previous step. Tap lightly with one or two fingers but briskly 3-5 times.

Next, you'll tap each of the meridian points 5-7 times, or so as you don't need to count the taps, and move around the body in the following order while saying the statement or a shortened phrase (i.e., feeling anxious):

1. Top of head
2. Eyebrow
3. Side eye
4. Under eye
5. Under nose
6. Chin
7. Collarbone
8. Underarm

Once you have gone through the sequence, you'll go back to the side of hand and repeat the statement or shortened phrase while tapping 15-20 times. Then take three deep breaths breathing in through your nose and out through your mouth.

Review and Re-rate the Issue or Problem

Once you have completed the tapping sequence, it's time to review how you're feeling. Refer back to the scoring scale of one to ten and determine where you are now and compare it to where you were previously.

The goal is to get you to be three or less on the scale. If you're still scoring high or want to go lower, you can do the sequence again.

One of my preferred methods is to repeat the entire tapping sequence three times before moving to the final meridian point, where I'm tapping the side of my hand 15-20 times to close the session.

Lastly, if you're feeling adventurous there is an optional closing procedure you can implement and it's called the Nine Gamut Treatment. It's simple to do and you would initiate it after you finalize the last tapping sequence on the side of the hand. See the steps below:

1. Close the eyes
2. Open the eyes
3. Look down and to the right then bring eyes back to the center
4. Look down and to the left then bring eyes back to the center
5. Roll eyes around clockwise
6. Roll eyes around counterclockwise
7. Hum 'Happy Birthday' for five seconds
8. Count from 1-5 out loud
9. Count from 5-1 out loud
10. Hum 'Happy Birthday' for five seconds

And there you have it! One simplified way to practice EFT yourself. I cannot wait for you to give this healing modality a try, as I know firsthand how powerful it can be. Not only do I use this on myself, but I am also practicing with my son, so yes, it is safe to do with your children too. If they are struggling with grief and loss due to a significant change in their life, I encourage you to use this healing method on them too.

If you are interested in using EFT with your child and on the younger side, I recommend you use affirmations instead of a statement discussing an issue or problem.

Below are the affirmations I use with my son when I need to redirect his focus, balance his energy and assist in calming him down. Sometimes I'll choose one that we repeat as we tap, and other times we use one on each tapping point. It just all depends on the situation and his willingness to participate.

- I am brave.
- I am strong.
- I am confident.
- I am kind.
- I am smart.
- I am unique.
- I am special.
- I am loved.

For the statement, I use a modified version such as, *"Even though I feel _____ {insert issue or problem} right now, I'm an awesome kid!"*

Here is an example for you: Even though I feel angry right now, I am an awesome kid!

To conclude, I hope you found value in learning more about EFT for you (and your family). The next alternative and holistic healing method to explore is nutrition. Odd? Perhaps, but not if you believe that food has medicinal properties to it. Let's explore this topic more together.

Nutrition

I would be remiss if I didn't talk briefly about your nutrition and the foods you eat. Yes, foods can impact how you handle your grief and loss.

For starters, your body needs the proper nutrients to function optimally. Grief, in and of itself, takes a toll on the body and one's overall wellness. Not eating the right foods to fuel your body can have adverse effects on your mental, emotional, and physical health.

One of the things I see often is stress or emotional eating. While this tends to be a go-to process for many that are grieving, it's also unhealthy. I have also seen and experienced first-hand binge eating. There were days I would eat non-stop, and then there were days I would barely eat anything. Overall, it's not healthy.

Now, I do not claim to be a nutritionist or a health coach, but I do know enough to understand how food can be used as medicine to support us when we are grieving.

With that said, I want to share some tidbits of information with you. Take with it what you may, and I recommend you speak with a professional about your diet while grieving if you have underlying medical conditions or need extra support.

First and foremost, you need to eat. It was challenging for me to eat larger meals most days, so I focused on eating several small meals throughout the day and enjoyed healthy snacks.

In full transparency, eating healthy and getting control of the foods I was putting into my body didn't happen until I was ready to heal from my grief. Therefore, if you are anything like me and grabbing for comfort foods or are binge eating, know that I did it too.

Show yourself some grace. You just went through something potentially traumatic and life-changing. We do what we can to cope, and I will not shame you for that. However, I do want you to acknowledge that it's likely not healthy and that gaining control over your health while you grieve is essential.

The key is to improve your eating habits as part of a lifestyle change, not a fad "diet." This lifestyle change will support you emotionally, mentally, physically, and in my opinion, even spiritually when grieving, and of course, afterward, too. The goal is to make a conscious and mindful effort to choose various nutritious foods in the right amounts for you. Make these choices part of your everyday routine.

I won't tell you that you need to eat six meals a day because the truth is your body is unique. The amount of meals you eat per day and how many calories you consume is out of my realm and area of expertise, so I recommend working with someone specializing in this field.

However, I will tell you to eat regularly. The last thing I wanted to fixate on was worrying about eating every couple of hours or counting calories while trying to heal and process my grief. I needed it to be simple not to overwhelm my mind and cause me to spiral with my depression and anxiety. I say that so you know where my headspace was at the time. Keeping it simple was the name of the game for me.

While we feel the stressors of a significant life change and the impacts of grief, it's often a natural response to crave comfort foods, desserts, and other sugary items, like soda. Many of these foods cause inflammation and wreak havoc on our bodies which impacts us as a whole.

Rather than grabbing for the foods that aren't optimal for our health, instead focus on eating the colors of the rainbow. I truly believe that food is medicine when you eat the right types of foods, that is.

When we focus on eating the colors of the rainbow, we can ensure our bodies are getting a variety of nutrients. Not only that, but if we look at our chakra system, we can also support our energetic body system to stay balanced by eating foods that help each of the chakras. When we know or sense a particular chakra is out of alignment, eating foods that associate with the chakra's color can dispel excess energy or remove any energetic blockages allowing the chakra to spin as it should and balance out.

Therefore, let's briefly discuss foods that you can eat that'll not only provide your body with optimal nutrition but will also help balance and align your chakra system.

Root Chakra

The root chakra or the first chakra is associated with the color red. Therefore, eating foods red in color can support this chakra. Some foods to consider are strawberries, red apples, pomegranates, raspberries, tomatoes, radishes, and beets, to name a few. You can also consider spices such as paprika and cayenne.

Sacral Chakra

The sacral chakra or the second chakra is associated with the color orange. Eating foods orange in color will offer support in healing this particular chakra. Therefore, some foods to consider are mangos, oranges, peaches, apricots, sweet potatoes, carrots, orange peppers, almonds or walnuts, and salmon. A spice to consider eating is cinnamon.

Solar Plexus Chakra

The solar plexus chakra or third chakra is associated with the color yellow. Thereby eating foods yellow in color will offer this chakra support. Some foods to consider are banana, pineapple, lemons, corn, yellow peppers, oats or brown rice, and curry as a spice.

Heart Chakra

The heart chakra or the fourth chakra is associated with the color green. As previously discussed, this is the chakra that needs the most TLC when grieving. Therefore, focusing your attention here and consider eating kiwis, green apples, limes, avocado, kale, broccoli, spinach, chard, dandelion greens, parsley, peas, celery, cucumber, zucchini, matcha, green tea, and spirulina.

Throat Chakra

The throat chakra or the fifth chakra is associated with the color blue. Eating foods blue in color will offer this chakra support. Consider eating blackberries, blueberries, and plums.

Brow or Third Eye Chakra

The brow or third eye chakra is the sixth chakra, and it's associated with the color indigo or purple. Consider eating purple grapes, purple kale, purple cabbage, eggplant, purple carrots, and cacao to offer this chakra support.

Crown Chakra

The crown chakra or the seventh chakra is associated with the color white. Therefore, fasting or juicing is recommended, and drinking plenty of fluids to aid in detoxifying the body.

As a side note, you can also incorporate essential oils into the mix. I believe some essential oils are safe to ingest and following safety guidelines is imperative. However, if you are not comfortable ingesting essential oils, you can inhale or use them topically. See the section on Aromatherapy for some guidelines to follow. Choose oils that correspond to each chakra color that will offer the chakras support for balancing and aiding in supporting your healing.

Lastly, I previously shared with you in **Chapter 4 - Developing a Warrior Mindset**, my daily mindset routine, and part of that was my healthy lifestyle change. You can review that section again for the specifics of my dietary changes.

Sound Therapy

Sound therapy or sound healing is a complementary or alternative medicine therapy. As with color therapy, not all medical professionals believe in these alternative methods.

In my opinion, it's a shame because so many available options genuinely have healing capabilities. But I get it; I was once a skeptic until I experienced the benefits first hand and can affirm they don't offer a placebo effect either.

What is sound therapy?

Sound therapy is where a person uses sound to treat physical and mental conditions by using instruments or the human voice to send sound waves and harmonic vibrations to the body for healing.

What are the benefits of sound therapy?

Sound therapy offers support and provides relief of both physical and psychological pain.

How can you utilize sound therapy in your life to support your healing journey?

It's pretty easy. Some certified practitioners provide sound therapy as part of their practice. However, you can also leverage the internet, such as

YouTube, where you'll find many videos with Tibetan bowls, binaural beats, and more.

As mentioned previously, the heart needs the most healing when dealing with grief, no matter the type of loss. Therefore, finding music that supports that area for healing is imperative.

Per an article with Eterneva, they state the following: *"Different philosophies and religions, like Buddhism and Hinduism, have found that the 432 frequency works well with the heart. Love, warmth, compassion and joy are all located there, so the sound waves have a positive influence on the mental and spiritual health of the listener."*[17]

I encourage you to explore different types of music and sounds to determine what resonates with you. Perhaps it'll be binaural beats, sounds of nature, bells chiming, or even classical music. There is no one size fits all approach here, and you'll have to be open to exploring different options.

Now that we have discussed various alternative and holistic methods to supporting yourself while overcoming significant life-changing situations and grief, let's delve into how to unleash the warrior within right after you complete the Action Step below.

***

Action Step: Choose a couple of healing modalities to commit to using daily for at least a week before deciding if you want to change or add another modality to your routine. Give yourself a score before and after a healing session, with one being the lowest and ten being the highest— record in a journal your healing activities, thoughts, emotions, pain daily, and score. Monitor your progress and evaluate what is working and eliminate what isn't. Consistency is the key to successfully adapting to changes. It takes at least 21 days to form a new habit, so please don't rush this process. Be patient.

Chapter 7 - Unleashing the Warrior Within

Unleashing your inner warrior is about tapping into your inner strength and harnessing its power, your personal power!

I have some basic rules for unleashing the warrior within; let's explore them briefly.

1. Tune in and follow your intuition
2. Eliminate the toxicity in your life (people, places, things, chemicals, etc.)
3. Ditch the victim mentality and negative mindset
4. Get clear on your values, mission, and goals
5. Heal wounds from the past
6. Make yourself a priority
7. Set aside time to be playful
8. Do more of what brings you joy
9. Ask for what you need
10. Find balance and stillness within your life

All of the above are guidelines and, for the most part, simple enough to follow. However, I want to discuss more in-depth processes to support you in unleashing your inner warrior.

Here is what we are going to delve further into:

1. Chakras
2. Mindful Meditation
3. Setting Boundaries

To start, let's review chakras!

Chakras

In **Chapter 6 - Utilizing Alternative & Holistic Healing Methods,** we discussed energy healing and briefly reviewed the chakras. When we look at unleashing our power, the chakra most impacted is the solar plexus or third chakra.

While it is crucial to have all of your chakras balanced, and there are various ways to do that, we will only discuss the solar plexus chakra, for now, to keep things simple. You're welcome to review Chapter 6 for more detailed information about the other chakras.

With that said, let's delve into the solar plexus chakra! As a reminder, this chakra is associated with the color yellow.

Use the following exercise and list to determine if your solar plexus chakra is out of alignment and needs balancing. If you mark yes with three or more symptoms, you could benefit from giving this chakra some attention to help you tap into your personal power, boost your confidence, and balance your energy.

When your chakra is underactive, it means it's likely blocked, weak, and has low energy. Below are some symptoms to identify if your solar plexus is underactive.

Underactive Symptoms:

- Feelings of low self-esteem
- Feeling a lack of self-trust
- Experiencing slow digestion
- Experiencing a victim mentality
- Unable to take responsibility
- Feeling an attraction to stimulants
- Giving too much of yourself

- Lacking confidence in self
- Unable to stand up for yourself
- Experiencing low energy

When your chakra is overactive, it means it's likely out of control and has too much energy. Below are some symptoms to identify if your solar plexus is overactive.

Overactive Symptoms:

- Being overly aggressive
- Feelings a need to be right
- Experiencing fast digestion
- Having a narrow or fixed mindset
- Feeling an attraction to sedatives
- Taking on too much responsibility
- Feeling overly competitive
- Inability to trust others
- Experiencing hyperactivity

It doesn't matter whether you find three or more symptoms under the underactive or overactive categories or a combination between the two; it's an indicator that your chakra needs attention for balancing. As mentioned, there are numerous ways to balance your chakras; choose options that align with you. However, if you need some ideas, take a look at the following suggestions:

Guided Meditation

Find a meditation that focuses on the solar plexus chakra or mindful practice meditation.

We will discuss mindful meditation as part of the next step to unleashing the warrior within.

Crystals

As previously mentioned, crystals have remarkable healing properties. Sit with clear quartz, kyanite, or any yellow stones such as tiger's eye, yellow calcite, pyrite, and citrine for 10-15 minutes and place it where the solar plexus chakra is located, under your belly button.

Aromatherapy

You can utilize several aromatherapy options to balance the chakras, but my favorite is to use essential oils. You may diffuse, inhale, or apply topically with a carrier oil yellow inspired oils. These would include bergamot, cypress, roman chamomile, geranium, juniper berry, lemon, rosemary, or sandalwood.

However, a word of caution is to be mindful of which oils you are using, as some can be phototoxic, like bergamot and lemon.

Food

Food is medicine and, therefore, can balance your chakras. Eat various foods such as bananas, pineapple, corn, lemons, squash, yellow peppers, oats, brown rice, or anything yellow in color.

As mentioned, you can choose one or more of these suggestions to support you in balancing your chakra. Trust your intuition.

Next, we will be discussing mindful meditation and how it can be a catalyst to healing your chakra but has numerous other benefits for your overall health and wellbeing. It's a game-changer, in my opinion!

Mindful Meditation

As part of your healing journey and tapping into your inner power, incorporating mindful meditation is a crucial component and, in my opinion, the foundation for your healing, growth, and transformation.

There are several benefits to meditation; in fact, there are irrefutable science-based facts! According to Healthline Media[1], the science-backed benefits include:

- Reduces stress
- Controls anxiety
- Promotes emotional health
- Supports self-awareness
- Increases mental clarity, focus, and attention span
- Reduces memory loss
- Aids in fighting addiction
- Promotes love and kindness
- Improves sleep
- Supports pain management
- Decrease blood pressure
- Promotes overall better health

Additionally, it can balance your chakras and improve your overall well-being!

Meditation is free, doesn't require any equipment or special props, specific location, or skill level. Anyone can do it!

What is mindfulness?

Mindfulness is a state of being consciously aware of something from a nonjudgmental lens, and it's intentional. Therefore, it is essential to be mindful of your surroundings and the situation that is causing you to experience negative emotions when it comes to emotional management.

Mindfulness is also often associated with intention, awareness, observation, and acceptance. Let's explore these further.

Intention

Intention is about focusing on the present moment without thinking about past or future events.

Awareness

Awareness is about tuning into your five senses intentionally and mindfully to what is happening in the present moment.

Observation

Observation is about recognizing the world around you with your five senses and tuning into the positive and negative thoughts, sensations, or feelings that arise, observing them without reaction or judgment, and acknowledging them for what they are.

Acceptance

Acceptance is about accepting what you can or cannot control, and that includes what you may be experiencing through your five senses, without trying to change it, your reactions, or with judgment.

Since we are talking about meditation and mindfulness, we also need to discuss mindful meditation.

What is mindful meditation?

Mindful meditation typically involves breathing exercises, mental imagery or visualization, awareness of your body, mind, and five senses to promote body relaxation. The goal is to slow down racing thoughts, release negative emotions or feelings, calm your mind and body.

It doesn't require any fancy equipment, but if you want to use candles, essential oils, crystals, etc., you're welcome to add them to the meditation process. As for preparation, you need a comfortable place to sit, five minutes of free time, and a judgment-free mindset.[1]

How do you meditate?

Let's explore how to do that by using the step-by-step guide to mindful meditation below.

1. Find a comfortable place to sit that feels calm and relaxing for you.
2. Determine how long you plan to meditate. If you're a beginner, choose a shorter time frame, such as 3-5 minutes. Use a timer to focus on the task at hand and not worry about the time.
3. Close your eyes and ground yourself using the 5-4-3-2-1 grounding technique widely recognized and used by psychologists and behavioral specialists (with a slight twist).
   - Five things you SEE.
   - Four things you FEEL.
   - Three things you HEAR.
   - Two things you SMELL.
   - One POSITIVE thing about yourself, your situation, or your surroundings.
4. Set an intention and say a prayer.
5. Notice your body and its state.
6. Slow your breathing and inhale for three counts and exhale for three counts.
7. Follow the sensation of the breath as you inhale and exhale.

8. Say RAM slowly, which is the sound for the solar plexus chakra to help you stay in a meditative state. It can be done in your head, as a whisper, or out loud to yourself.
9. Notice when your mind wanders and redirect your focus to breathing.
10. Close with kindness and gratitude by making a note of your surroundings, how you feel, what you're grateful for, etc.

These are the basics of meditation, mindfulness, and mindful meditation. Mindfulness is something you can do throughout your day. Make a note of when you are present in the moment and when your attention is elsewhere. It'll help you zero in on where to redirect your time and attention to people, places, things, etc. that are important to you.

My recommendation is that you set aside time daily to practice mindful meditation. Start with 3-5 minutes and grow from there. The more you engage in this practice, the longer you will be able to meditate.

Next, let's review how setting healthy boundaries is another powerful component of standing in your power!

Setting Boundaries

Boundaries are the emotional, intellectual or mental, physical, and spiritual limits to how others can treat you, behave around you, as well as what they can expect from you.

Boundaries allow you to define, create, and maintain the space you need to show up as your highest and best self. Setting and enforcing your limits may not always come easily or naturally, but I promise practice makes progress, and with consistency, it will get more comfortable over time.

My husband often reminds me that what is common sense isn't always common knowledge. Therefore, I feel it's imperative that I spend a little more time on this topic and discuss its importance, types of boundaries and how to set them. In my opinion, boundaries are crucial to standing in your power and reclaiming your life!

These are the top five reasons why it is vital to set and keep healthy boundaries.

1. Healthy relationships
2. Feel heard and listened to
3. Feel validated, appreciated, and valued
4. Respected and understood
5. Your needs are covered

With that said, boundaries to reflect upon and consider are as follows:

- Emotional - Feelings and emotions to specific situations, triggers, or topics
- Intellectual - Thoughts, opinions, values, and beliefs, or respect for others
- Physical - Physical space, comfort with touch, or physical needs
- Social - Friendships, pursuing social activities or hobbies
- Spiritual - Spiritual or religious beliefs, practices, or rituals

Setting boundaries can be challenging but not impossible to establish. Here is a quick seven-step guide to setting healthy boundaries to get you started.

1. Identify the boundaries or limitations you need.
2. Understand why you need those boundaries.
3. Never apologize for setting or enforcing your limits.
4. Be direct in communicating your boundaries to others.
5. Determine what happens if your boundaries are not respected.
6. Address how you will correspond to the person about the broken boundary.

7. Trust your gut and practice mindfulness to create awareness for your limitations.

I encourage you to go through all seven steps from above and outline the boundaries you need to make to take control over your life. When done, review the Action Step before moving onto the next chapter to discuss how to reclaim your life.

***

Action Step: Review each of the three steps to 'Unleashing the Warrior Within'. Take a journal and work through rewriting your story and exploring boundaries. This will help you organize your thoughts and provide clarity. Commit to practicing mindful meditation daily, even if it's only for a few minutes. Make it a habit because overall, it will help you and your healing in remarkable ways.

Chapter 8 - Reclaiming Your Life

When it comes to moving beyond the grief and reclaiming your life after loss, it genuinely doesn't have to be challenging. I see it often where friends, family, and clients get hung up on the details rather than stepping fully into who they have become due to their life-changing situation.

To start, ditching the victim mentality is imperative. If you did the exercises in **Chapter 4 - Developing a Warrior Mindset**, this should already be complete or currently being dealt with as part of your healing journey.

Next, let's discuss the four-step process to reclaim your life!

Step 1: Rewrite your story
Step 2: Rediscover yourself
Step 3: Embrace more joy
Step 4: Live your life unapologetically

It looks simple, right? In theory, yes. You can make this process as straightforward or as complicated as you want it to be. All right, time to break these steps down a bit further.

Rewrite Your Story

Rewriting your story essentially starts with ditching the victim mentality. From there, you want to reflect upon the stories you believe about yourself and challenge their existence.

Stories and beliefs shape our reality. What we believe and put energy behind can either empower or hinder us. John Assaraf said, *"The stories we tell ourselves shape our lives. They shape who we believe we are, and this belief translates into who we become."* Therefore, it is vital to acknowledge the power of our stories and the impact they have on our lives.

When you begin to identify and understand the stories you tell yourself, you can start to reclaim your life!

And that all starts with the power of choice. You can choose what stories you believe will empower you to move forward to the negative ones that'll hold you back.

We are natural storytellers, and we use them to communicate, connect, and make sense of the world around us. Our thoughts can manifest things to become a reality through the power of our intent, the energy behind our beliefs.

With that said, stories can come from various places, such as ancestral lineage, trauma, past experiences, negative habits or patterns, and other's beliefs or opinions.

Ancestral lineage stories are passed onto us over the years through the generations. Some were likely passed on for survival but have since become updated and are holding you back.

Trauma stories are fear-based and often created to feel safe, but it's essential to understand that the fear is not serving you positively and it's stopping your progress forward.

Past experience stories are the most common, and they're a way to hold onto the past. These experiences are often negative, and there tends to be regret involved. These stories hinder your future and your true potential.

Negative habits or pattern stories are about repetitive practices that we allow to define us and cause a negative mindset that holds us back from making the necessary changes to live a vibrant life.

Other people's beliefs or opinion stories are one's that don't belong to us, but we carry them around as baggage as if they do. Often coming from friends, family, colleagues, and those we find of influence. Accepting someone else's story as yours blocks our true potential and growth.

Moreover, it's crucial to reflect upon these stories and begin dismantling any that are not of truth or for your highest good.

How would you do something like that? Honestly, shadow work helps in this situation, but writing in a journal is beneficial too. For each story you wish to deconstruct, ask yourself the following questions:

1. What story am I telling myself that is holding me back?
2. Where did this story come from that I am telling myself? (i.e., ancestral lineage, others, etc.)
3. What self-limiting beliefs do I have about myself right now?
4. How are these beliefs influencing my life right now?
5. What, if anything, am I attracting or manifesting into my life with my beliefs, thoughts, and energy?
6. Is the story that I'm telling myself true?
7. Does this story empower me or disempower me?
8. Is this story serving me positively and for my highest good?
9. Is this story aligned with my true and Divine purpose?
10. What new thoughts and beliefs can I change to change the narrative of this story to be empowering?

Once you start unpacking the invisible baggage you've been lugging around, you can begin to see how much it's impacted your life, and you can make a conscious decision to choose to write your story. Change the narrative!

Rediscover Yourself

Rediscovering yourself is about reflecting upon who you are at your core. What makes you, you? Evaluate what brings positivity into your life, what you're passionate about, and your purpose.

I believe we all have a Divine purpose, some choose to answer the call, and others ignore it. I want to encourage you to explore who you are by peeling back the layers of your identity, healing the wounds still there, causing pain, and moving forward in life.

Once you can identify who you are beneath the exterior, you can then review and learn how to live your life with more joy.

Embrace More Joy

When it comes to embracing more joy, it's really just that—seeking and incorporating more fun into your life. What lights you up brighter than the sky on Independence day? Do more of it!

Want to take a course, get a degree or start a nonprofit? Super, do it!

Desire to change careers, adopt, or learn to paint? Awesome, do it!

Ready to travel the world, write a book, or start a business? Great, do it!

Life is far too short to be miserable. Create opportunities to bring more happiness and joy into your life. Start with one thing and add more over time. The results are worth it!

Live Your Life Unapologetically

Living your life unapologetically is about not apologizing for who you are, your past, the opinions or others, none of it. It's the ability to look at yourself in the mirror and say, "Damn, I look good! Let's slay the day!"

You are a force to be reckoned with; therefore, seize the opportunity to live your life loud and proud. Be you! Own your uniqueness and stand in your truth!

As we come to the end of this chapter, I want to encourage you to complete the Action Step below, as this final step in the framework is essential to your growth, healing, and transformation. When done, let's wrap things up with my final thoughts on everything we have discussed.

***

Action Step: Take a moment to review each step of the 'Reclaiming Your Life' process and journal through each of them. Take your time, pause, reflect, and write some more. The goal is to have greater awareness for who you are and how you want to live your life moving forward.

Chapter 9 - Final Thoughts

As we come to the closing of this book, I hope you enjoyed the content and found value in what I shared with you because what you hold within your hands is a simplified framework to overcome adversity, grief, and loss that I have used for myself and my clients.

If you commit to implementing the steps in this book with an open mind and heart, you will see progress. I cannot say it'll happen overnight as everyone has a different healing journey and timeline. However, I can say that if you are patient, consistent, and dedicated, healing will occur.

Lastly, know that you are not alone, and I empathize with the pain you are experiencing. If I can be of assistance in any way, please do not hesitate to connect with me. You will find my contact information at the back of the book in my author bio. I encourage you to reach out as I have a variety of ways to support you.

I'm sincerely sorry for the pain and loss you have experienced. May you move beyond the grief and reclaim your life after the loss. Cheers to your healing and transformation! I believe in you!

References

Chapter 2

1. Dryden-Edwards, MD, R. (n.d.). *Grief: Loss of a Loved One*. MedicineNet. Retrieved March 31, 2020, from https://www.medicinenet.com/loss_grief_and_bereavement/article.htm

Chapter 3

1. Robinson, L., Smith, M.A., M., & Segal, Ph.D., J. (2020, February). *Emotional and Psychological Trauma*. HelpGuide. Retrieved June 19, 2021, from https://www.helpguide.org/articles/ptsd-trauma/coping-with-emotional-and-psychological-trauma.htm

Chapter 4

1. *Zahariades, D. (2020). The Mental Toughness Handbook.*
2. *Neuro-Linguistic Programming (NLP).* (2018, February 8). GoodTherapy®. Retrieved July 2, 2021, from https://www.goodtherapy.org/learn-about-therapy/types/neuro-linguistic-programming

Chapter 5

1. Luna, A. (2021, June 21). *Shadow Work: The Ultimate Guide + Free Psychological Test*. Lonerwolf. Retrieved July 11, 2021, from https://lonerwolf.com/shadow-work-demons/

Chapter 6

1. Engel, M. (2014, July 18). Does energy healing really work? The Daily News puts four methods to the test. *Daily News.* https://www.nydailynews.com/life-style/health/energy-healing-work-article-1.1872210
2. Judith, A. (2018). *Wheels of Life.* (2nd Edition). Woodbury, MN: Llewellyn Publications.
3. Judith, A. (n.d.). *Chakra One.* Retrieved April 2, 2020, from https://anodeajudith.com/chakra-one/
4. Judith, A. (n.d.). *Chakra Two.* Retrieved April 2, 2020, from https://anodeajudith.com/chakra-two/
5. Judith, A. (n.d.). *Chakra Three.* Retrieved April 2, 2020, from https://anodeajudith.com/chakra-three/
6. Judith, A. (n.d.). *Chakra Four.* Retrieved April 2, 2020, from https://anodeajudith.com/chakra-four
7. Judith, A. (n.d.). *Chakra Five.* Retrieved April 2, 2020, from https://anodeajudith.com/chakra-five/
8. Judith, A. (n.d.). *Chakra Six.* Retrieved April 2, 2020, from https://anodeajudith.com/chakra-six/
9. Judith, A. (n.d.). *Chakra Seven.* Retrieved April 2, 2020, from https://anodeajudith.com/chakra-seven/
10. *What is Reiki.* (n.d.). The International Center for Reiki Training. Retrieved July 4, 2021, from https://www.reiki.org/faqs/what-reiki
11. Cronkleton, E. (2019, March 8). *Aromatherapy Uses and Benefits.* Healthline. Retrieved April 3, 2020, from https://www.healthline.com/health/what-is-aromatherapy
12. *10 Healing Benefits of Aromatherapy.* (n.d.). boom.boom®. Retrieved April 6, 2020, from https://boomboomnaturals.com/blogs/news/10-healing-benefits-of-aromatherapy
13. *Essential Oils Guide: Safety.* (n.d.). dōTERRA Essential Oils. Retrieved April 6, 2020, from https://www.doterra.com/US/en/blog/healthy-living-essential-oils-guide-safety

14. *The Essential Life* (3rd ed.). (2017). Total Wellness Publishing.

15. Hall, J. (2003). *The Crystal Bible: A Definitive Guide to Crystals.* (1st ed.). Walking Stick Press.

16. Anthony, K. (n.d.). *What is EFT tapping?* Healthline. Retrieved July 11, 2021, from https://www.healthline.com/health/eft-tapping

17. Wallace, T. (n.d.). *Sound Therapy for Grieving: The Heart Frequency and a Playlist*. Eterneva. Retrieved July 10, 2021, from https://eterneva.com/resources/sound-therapy-for-grief

Chapter 7

1. Thorpe, MD, PhD, M., & Link, MS, RD, R. (2017, July 5). *12 Science-Based Benefits of Meditation*. Healthline. Retrieved April 5, 2020, from https://www.healthline.com/nutrition/12-benefits-of-meditation

About the Author

Kayla Brissi is a multi-passionate entrepreneur, speaker, author, and the owner of Kayla Brissi LLC and Intuitive Spiritual Warrior Holistic Consulting & Healing LLC.

As a life transformation strategist, Kayla guides her clients to break free from limiting beliefs and stuck patterns by helping them unleash their inner warrior so they can regain control over their lives and live with more passion and purpose. Her mission is to transcend limits, break barriers, and transform lives!

Kayla has contributed to numerous industry publications and online platforms such as Thrive Global, Today, and Skillshare. In addition, FOX, NBC, CBS, MarketWatch, Digital Journal, and various other sites and digital magazines have featured Kayla, and multiple podcasts and radio shows have interviewed her over the years.

She is also the author of *Healing from Grief: Transform Your Pain Into Purpose and Honor Your Loved One* and *Transforming Inner Pain: Moving Beyond the Grief and Reclaiming Your Life After Loss* and the co-author of various anthologies: *The Beauty in My Mess: Stories of Truth, Transparencies and Triumphs, Driven: A Guidebook for Women by Women; To Inspire and Empower, Out of My Comfort Zone: Stories of Courage, Perseverance and Victory, Dust to Salvation: Stories of Grace, Love, and Redemption in the Midst of Jesus Revealing Unexpected Miracles*, and *Embracing the Journey: Inspiring Stories of Hope, Healing and Triumphing over Adversity*.

Kayla has a Masters in Business Administration with a concentration in finance and a Bachelor of Arts in Accounting and Business Administration from Lakeland University (formerly Lakeland College) and a Financial Services Technical Diploma from Mid-State Technical College.

She has also acquired various coaching, holistic healing, and spiritual certifications that have allowed her to provide unparalleled support for her clients regarding their transformation.

When Kayla's not writing her next best-selling book or helping her clients bulldoze through the proverbial locked doors, you can catch her eating ice cream, reading a book or watching a movie, and spending time with her family.

To learn more about Kayla, please visit her websites at intuitivespiritualwarrior.com and kaylabrissi.com.

Join the Community

If you would like to receive a notification when my next book releases, receive free book promotions, behind the scenes access, information about upcoming events, sales, and receive exclusive discounts, join my online community by visiting my websites at intuitivespiritualwarrior.com or kaylabrissi.com.

Review Request

Please leave a review on Amazon (and other online retailers)! The number of reviews a book accumulates daily has a direct impact on how well it sells. Therefore, leaving an honest and positive review, no matter its length, truly helps make it possible for me to continue releasing quality books.

For ease, you can leave your review on Amazon at https://www.amazon.com/dp/B08TFB1H5Y.

Other Books by Kayla Brissi

Healing from Grief: Transform Your Pain Into Purpose and Honor Your Loved One

Losing her father to cancer, Kayla wasn't prepared for the aftermath of his death. Struggling with depression, anxiety, and PTSD, her life was anything but perfect. Each day she tried to cope with his loss, process the roller coaster of emotions, and provide for her family while running multiple businesses. Ultimately it led to a breakdown that caused her life to unravel completely.

With perseverance, grit, and her faith, she fearlessly found her inner warrior and began to battle the demons of her life, pulled herself out of the depths of hell, and transformed her pain into her purpose.

Kayla met with medical professionals, alternative medical practitioners, spiritual healers, spent countless hours researching, educating, and implementing ideas to discover a better way to heal from grief.

Now, she aspires to share these secrets with you!

Explore within the book's pages how to Discover Your Inner Spiritual Warrior, Holistically Heal Yourself, and Turn Your Pain into Your Purpose.

May you, too, move forward beyond the tragedy, grief, and loss to a renewed life full of freedom, joy, and purpose!

Anthologies Co-Authored by Kayla Brissi

Driven: A Guidebook By Women For Women; To Inspire and Empower

Women all across the world have come together to share their knowledge, joys, and pains of business, love, parenting, self-care, goal setting, finances and more.

This guidebook leaves no stone unturned to help you find your will to reach greater heights. You'll be ready to stop giving room to excuses and instead, you'll be ready to push forward in your dreams and truly crush your goals.

Dust to Salvation: Stories of Grace, Love, and Redemption in the Midst of Jesus Revealing Unexpected Miracles

Seven women are sharing their innermost secrets of failed relationships, health scares, infertility, and single parenting and they were brought together with one common bond. The undying love of Jesus Christ and how their lives are filled with hope for the future.

Independently, they discovered through prayer and unexpected friendships there was life beyond the brokenness that enveloped their hearts.

Embracing the Journey: Inspiring Stories of Hope, Healing and Triumphing over Adversity

Over ten brave women came together with one mission in mind; to share their stories to inspire, empower, and offer hope and healing to those who may be experiencing something similar - grief and loss, divorce, toxic relationships and narcissism, abuse, addiction, mental health disorders, challenging health journeys, spiritual awakenings, being a parent of a child with special needs and intellectual disABILITIES, and more!

These empowering women learned to triumph over adversity, and as a result, they're stronger, wiser, and have a new perspective on life. Now they wish to share their wisdom with you.

Out of My Comfort Zone: Stories of Courage, Perseverance and Victory

Out of My Comfort Zone features profiles from remarkable women of all backgrounds and places in life. Explore stories from business coaches, a publishing consultant, professional life-style bloggers, a marketing strategist, and educators from across the globe. Each of these rising entrepreneurs offers valuable insight on the struggles, challenges and life-changing moments that brought them success and personal satisfaction.

These remarkable women took risks, sought out challenges, and persevered in the face of adversity. By leaning into their passions and drive for success, they were able to change their lives.

Now, they share those stories – and advice – with others. Out of My Comfort Zone is a must read for all women, no matter their personal journey. Learn how ordinary women navigated hurdles and found the courage, perseverance, and determination to push through to beat the odds.

The Beauty in My Mess: Stories of Truth, Transparencies and Triumphs (Vol I)

Over thirty courageous women joined together to tell a small piece of their autobiography that had a profound impact on their lives.

Within these pages, the authors have poured their hearts and souls into their stories by unveiling a time in their life where they had to find the deep inner strength, faith, and determination to see the beauty in their mess. They are stories of pain, healing, perseverance, and victory.

They are their stories for HIS glory!